W9-COE-227

"A fascinating look at Egyptian mummies and the science of exploration through which modern investigators have learned about them . . . will send many readers to the museums and bookshelves to learn more."

—(starred review) *ALA Booklist*

"Comprehensive and serves the double function of fulfilling curriculum needs as well as being excellent recreational reading fare. Historical research is well-documented, drawings are graphically excellent, but it is the fluid style and the focus on obscure detail that makes the book so engrossing and immediate."

—(starred review) *Children's Book Review Service*

"Egyptian mummification is thoroughly presented along with brief mention of other kinds of body preservation after death."

—(starred review) *Library Journal*

"[There is] no lack of the shivery appeal which makes mummies universally popular."

—*The Kirkus Reviews*

MILDRED MASTIN PACE is the author of an award-winning biography of Clara Barton; *My Japan,* written with Hiroko Nakamoto; and *Old Bones the Wonder Horse,* a story which won the Dorothy Canfield Fisher award. She and her husband live in Garrison, New York, where Mrs. Pace is active in the affairs of the local library.

THE LAUREL-LEAF LIBRARY brings together under a single imprint outstanding works of fiction and non-fiction particularly suitable for young adult readers, both in and out of the classroom. This series is under the editorship of Charles F. Reasoner, Professor of Elementary Education, New York University.

Mildred Mastin Pace

Wrapped for Eternity
The Story of the Egyptian Mummy

Egyptologist and Content Consultant
Kenneth Jay Linsner
Line drawings by Tom Huffman

Published by
Dell Publishing Co., Inc.
1 Dag Hammarskjold Plaza
New York, New York 10017

Laurel-Leaf Library ® TM 766734, Dell Publishing Co., Inc.

ISBN: 0-440-98886-1

Reprinted by arrangement with McGraw-Hill Book Company
Printed in the United States of America

First Laurel printing—January 1976
Second Laurel printing—April 1978

To Clark,

my best critic

and favorite proofreader

Acknowledgments

Though the subject is ancient, much of the help I got on this book came from young people. The idea—a book on Egyptian mummies—was that of a young editor, Leigh Dean, then at McGraw-Hill. She introduced me to an Egyptologist in his early twenties, Kenneth Jay Linsner, who knew a great deal about Egyptian mummies. (He even unwrapped one—see Chapter 8.)

Mr. Linsner then opened the door for me to a researcher's paradise: the Wilbour Library of Egyptology at the Brooklyn Museum, one of the world's greatest collections of books on ancient Egypt. There Eleanor Wedge, the librarian, and her staff of young people gave me the kind of eager, knowledgeable help that made research so exciting and rewarding. It was difficult at long last, to leave them and start the actual writing.

Once the writing began, Kenneth Linsner again was a tremendous source of help and information. When I queried, he more than answered. He corrected, illuminated, and amplified. Even when he was in Egypt on a dig, my questions—and his long replies —literally flew back and forth.

Others were of great service too, sharing material and information. Not the least of these was the Butterfield Memorial Library in Cold Spring, New York, a member of Mid-Hudson Libraries, whose staff was ever willing to track down hard-to-get books and check sources. To them all, my thanks.

But especially my deepest gratitude goes to Kenneth Jay Linsner, Eleanor Wedge and her staff, and to Leigh Dean who gave me steady encouragement and support during the two years I worked writing this book.

Mildred Mastin Pace

Contents

Foreword

Speak! for thou long enough has acted dummy,
Thou hast a tongue—come—let us hear its tune;
Thou'rt standing on thy legs, above ground, mummy,
Revisiting the glimpses of the moon,
Not like thin ghosts, or disembodied creatures,
But with thy bones, and flesh, and limbs and features.

The above is a fragment of a long poem first published in the *London Morning Chronicle* of February 18, 1835. Written by a "Mr. Campbell" and entitled "Address to the Mummy," it represents that period's romantic attitude toward the "preserved mortal remains of human beings who were inhabitants of this earth more than 3,000 years ago." Although it has long since lost its power to stir us and may even seem comical, it does provide us with a glimpse into the spirit of inquiry that permeated the age. This spirit is still alive today.

The cry "Speak!" was raised not so much out of a silence on the part of antiquity, but rather out of an inability to hear clearly. In this book an attempt is made to relate what we have learned about ancient Egyptian religion and life by improving our old "listening" techniques and by developing new ones.

Ancient Egypt has, for all practical purposes, always aroused great curiosity and interest. Beginning with the writings of the father of history, Herodotus, in the fifth century b.c., through today's popular texts, certain main strands of this interest may be picked out. Of these, two can be said to have provoked more general concern than any others: pyramidology and "mummiology."

Pyramidology, or the study of pyramids—particularly those of the Giza plateau—has perhaps reached a dead end today, since its main purpose was the divining of the astral and timeless secrets of these monuments.

The "secrets" of the pyramids, as revealed by earlier savants, gained them the nickname of Pyramidiots. Today our scientific investigations have dispelled much of this earlier "wisdom" and moved us closer to a real understanding of ancient Egyptian civilization.

The second strand of interest is that which we deal with in this book: the study of mummies. Although the period of "mummidiocy" is long and extremely interesting, one must not lose perspective on the subject. Our study of dried human remains should be seen within the larger picture of the investigation of the funerary arts and crafts of ancient Egypt, including architecture and wall decoration. Only through the study of what the ancient Egyptians have left us, and this by and large is funereal in nature, can we possibly recapture what their civilization was like. This legacy includes their mummified bodies.

What becomes immediately apparent in such a study is that the ancient Egyptians loved life and living. This book is meant to reflect this aspect as well, for it is the true value of any such work. The Egyptians loved life so much that they thought of the afterworld as a copy of this one, a perpetuation of this life. In the words of a funeral song of 1200 B.C.: "O Grave thou art built for festivity, thou art founded for what is fair."

It is thus by a detailed study of their thoughts about and beliefs for the afterlife, as manifested in writing, stone, and household artifacts, that a clear picture of what their life was like can be built up.

There is an old maxim: One never sees more

13

than one knows. This may be amended to read: One never *hears* more than one knows. Anytime you encounter an antiquity—be it a work of fine art, an ancient household utensil, a child's toy, or a mummy—it is saying something about the civilization that created it. It is up to you to listen.

Kenneth Jay Linsner
Institute of Fine Arts
New York University

Conservator-in-Chief, Boston Museum of Fine Arts/
Yale University Giza Project
Former Consultant, The Department of Egyptian
and Classical Art, The Brooklyn Museum

Map of ancient Egypt.

14

A CHRONOLOGY OF EGYPT'S KINGS

	DATES	NAMES		DATES	NAMES
THE OLD KINGDOM	1st & 2nd DYNASTY 2995-2635 B.C.	Menes (Narmer)	**THE NEW KINGDOM**	18th DYNASTY 1554-1305 B.C.	*Ahmose (Amosis I) *Amenhotep I (Amenophis I) *Tuthmosis I Tuthmosis II Hatshepsut Tuthmosis III Amenhotep II Tuthmosis IV Amenhotep III Amenhotep IV Semenkare *Tutankhamen *Queen Ankhesenamun Ay Horemhab
	3rd DYNASTY 2635-2570 B.C.	*Djoser (Zoser) *Imhotep, the Vizier			
	4th DYNASTY 2570-2450 B.C.	Snefru *Cheops (Khufu) *Hetepheres Chephren Mycerinus Shepseskaf			
	5th DYNASTY 2450-2290 B.C.	Userkaf Sahure		19th DYNASTY 1305-1196 B.C.	Ramesses I Seti I *Ramesses II *Lord Ameni Merenptah Seti II Siptah
	6th DYNASTY 2290-2155 B.C.	Pepi I Pepi II			
	7th-10th DYNASTY 2155-2040 B.C.	First Intermediate Period		20th DYNASTY 1196-1080 B.C.	*Ramesses III *Pawar *Ramesses IV Ramesses V *Ramesses VI Ramesses VII-IX
THE MIDDLE KINGDOM	11th DYNASTY 2134-1991 B.C.	*Meket-Re Mentuhotep I " II " III " IV *Horuta		21st DYNASTY 1080-946 B.C.	*High Priestess Makare *Count Pa-seba-khai-en-ipet
				22nd-26th DYNASTY 946-525 B.C.	
	12th DYNASTY 1991-1785 B.C.	Amenemhet I Sesostris I Amenemhet II Sesostris II " III Amenemhet III (Ammenemes III) " IV *Aty *Princess Senebtisi		27th DYNASTY 525-404 B.C.	Persian Domination *Herodotus
				28th-30th DYNASTY 404-342 B.C.	
	13th-15th DYNASTY 1785-1650 B.C.	Second Intermediate Period		PTOLEMAIC PERIOD 323-30 B.C.	Alexander the Great Ptolemy I-XII Cleopatra I-VII
	16th DYNASTY 1650-1554 B.C.	Hyksos Domination from Lower Egypt		ROMAN PERIOD 30 B.C. 7th Century A.D.	Augustin-Justinian
	17th DYNASTY 1650-1554 B.C.	Kamose *Seqenenre II (Upper Egypt)			

*Names to look for in the text

Events in ancient Egypt are dated by Dynasties. Each Dynasty represents the rule of a king and his direct descendants. The 1st Dynasty began with the rule of Menes, the earliest-known king of Egypt, in 3,000 B.C. The last Dynasty, the 30th, ended when Alexander the Great took over Egypt in 332 B.C. and the rule of Egypt by Egyptians was ended.

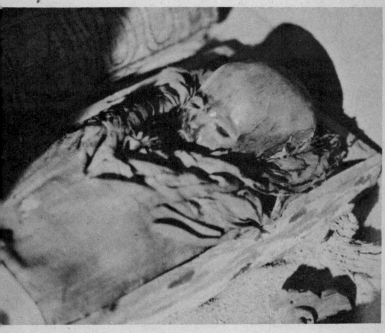

The mummy of a young child from Thebes rests in a plain wooden mummy case, her toys on the ground beside it. The University Museum, Philadelphia.

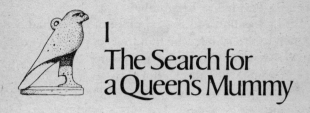

1
The Search for a Queen's Mummy

For more than four thousand years the second burial place of the Egyptian queen Hetepheres had remained a mystery.

Somewhere in this land of heat and sand and bleak rock cliffs the secret tomb was buried.

Over the centuries tomb robbers had searched and searched. To find it would mean wealth beyond a man's wildest dreams. For the queen had been buried with furniture of gold, and within the wrappings of her mummy were fortunes in jewelry and amulets of silver, gold, and precious stones.

They searched the endless expanse of desert, with its deep hot sands shifted by scorching winds.

But the desert gave no clues. They scaled the desolate cliffs and swept the hot sand from barren rocks looking for a sealed crack, some sign of a door that might lead to a passageway. But they never found an opening that led to her tomb.

The location of her first place of burial had been known to thousands: the hundreds of people who had walked behind the queen's mummy in the funeral procession to her tomb, the throngs who stood for miles along the hot, dusty roads of Dahshūr to watch the procession pass by.

She had been buried with pomp and splendor, as befitted a well-loved queen, the mother of the ruler of all Egypt, the great Pharaoh Khufu.

While Khufu mourned his mother's death, he was proud of the magnificence of her burial. And true to the religious beliefs of his time, he was comforted by it.

The coffin that held her mummy rested in a beautifully carved sarcophagus of the whitest alabaster. The burial chamber in which it stood was deep in the tomb, safe, he was sure, at the end of a series of stairs and passageways. The chamber, with its lavishly painted walls, had been sealed off so no one could ever enter it. Sealed off, too, were the nearby rooms that held the treasures and useful objects she would want and need in her new life in the next world.

Khufu thought with pride of the splendors of his

mother's burial—the magnificent furniture, the bed sheathed in heavy gold foil with its canopy of gold, the gold carrying chair, the armchair of gold; of the chests inlaid with gold and semiprecious stones that held her clothes, her toilet articles of gold, the elegant alabaster jars filled with precious oils and ointments.

All these and other treasure, too, were sealed away in the darkness of the tomb never to be disturbed in this world, only to be used by Queen Hetepheres in her afterlife.

In addition to closing off the burial chamber, blocking it with heavy stones, and sealing the other rooms, Khufu had priests and guards on watch day and night to protect his mother's tomb—and especially the burial chamber—from thieves.

Then one day a trusted employee came to him, terrified, to say the tomb, and the burial chamber itself, had been broken into. In rage and anguish Khufu questioned the man. The Pharaoh was assured that the sarcophagus had not been touched, the mummy was undisturbed, no damage had been done in the rooms of the tomb.

But these were corrupt times in Egypt, and Khufu was afraid there might be others bold enough to break into the tomb. He must move his mother's body to a safer place.

With the help of a few highly trusted people he found a place, remote and cleverly concealed. In great secrecy the alabaster sarcophagus, the golden furniture, and other treasured objects were moved into it. No one knows how this was done. Probably each piece was wrapped to disguise it, then piece by piece all were moved, under cover of darkness, by the trusted few.

With his queen-mother safely hidden in a new tomb, Khufu was able to concentrate, once again, on the tremendous project he had set for his lifetime: the building of his own tomb, the Great Pyramid at Giza.

Where graverobbers from ancient days on through the centuries searched for the second tomb of Queen Hetepheres and failed to find it, modern archeologists succeeded.

It was discovered more than four thousand years later because a photographer setting up a tripod for his camera on flat, sand-covered rock noticed that one leg of the tripod sank slightly into the surface. Now the average photographer might have taken no notice of such a small detail. But everyone connected with a serious archeological "dig" is trained to observe everything scrupulously. The tiniest detail is never overlooked.

This photographer was with an American archeological team known as the Harvard-Boston Expedition, which was headed by the noted archeologist George A. Reisner. They were working in Giza, near the Great Pyramid King Khufu had built.

Most of the time their work was routine and tedious. For days they had been methodically scooping through the sand, clearing down to native rock, scrutinizing every inch—and working without much hope. For the area had been gone over many times before.

The work was not easy. It was hot; when a breeze blew, it carried small blasts of sand, and insects swarmed in the still air.

Dull as the job might be, it was done faithfully: everything measured, recorded, photographed, day after day.

Then the one leg of the tripod sank slightly into a soft spot. Why? In what? Not rock!

It was a patch of plaster.

The men cleared the sand away and found it was rather a large patch. Still working slowly, recording and measuring, they removed the plaster and came upon a crudely dug, very steep, deep shaft blocked by regular masonry. It was not easy to remove these blocks and to climb down, though there were rough-hewn footholds hollowed out on one side of the shaft. With flashlights to help them down through the dank pitch-darkness, one by one, several of the men descended. One hundred feet down, they measured it.

At the bottom they found a burial chamber which they opened. Their lights flashed onto a great glow of gold. There were strips and lengths and sheets of solid gold, helter-skelter, piled on the floor of the chamber. Amongst the gold items they saw cluttered scraps of decayed wood.

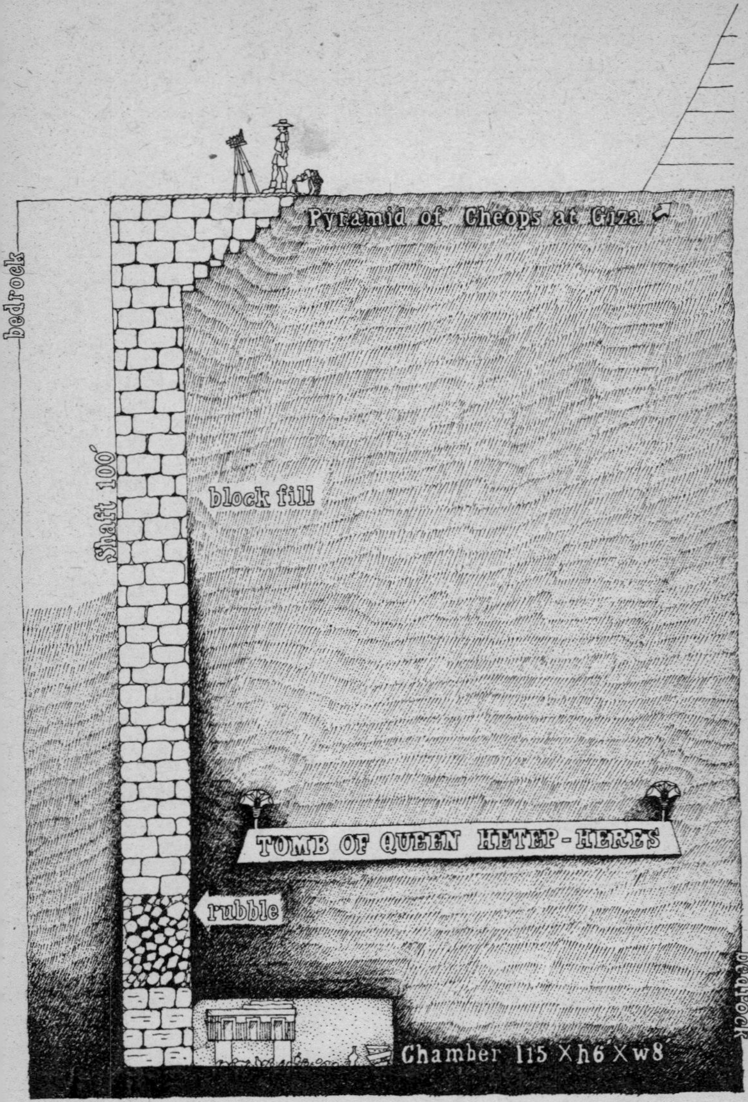

bedrock

Shaft 100′

block fill

Pyramid of Cheops at Giza

TOMB OF QUEEN HETEP-HERES

rubble

Chamber 115 × h6 × w8

bedrock

Amid the awesome disorder stood a beautiful sarcophagus, carved of alabaster, whole, gleaming white, and unmarked by time. They had found the second tomb of Queen Hetepheres, mother of Khufu, the tomb her son had hidden so well.

The gold sheets and strips were her golden furniture. Termites had eaten the wood and the furniture had collapsed. It would take many years and great patience, ingenuity, and skill, but eventually each piece would be reconstructed; each piece would look exactly as it had when carried to the queen's tomb.

Systematically the tedious job of clearing the burial chamber began. Not until everything else was safely removed would the sarcophagus be opened.

Meantime, the sarcophagus was the center of excited concern among archeologists all over the world. In this sarcophagus would be found the mummy of a queen who had lived in the 4th Dynasty, 2,500 years before Christ. No true mummy dating that far back had ever been found before.

And since she was an important queen, jewelry and amulets of rare beauty and great interest would have been buried with her.

The day came for the sarcophagus to be opened. Hundreds would have liked to witness it. But the

The second tomb of Queen Hetepheres.

burial chamber was so small, there was room for only eight people, and they were carefully chosen.

To get the eight archeologists and high officials down the steep shaft, a chair was rigged up on a pulley. One by one they were taken down.

They stood together, silent, tense with excitement, each man knowing it might be hours before they actually saw the mummy. For within the sarcophagus there should be two, perhaps three, beautifully painted coffins, fitted one inside the other, the innermost containing the mummy of the queen. Each would have to be opened with time-consuming caution and skill to avoid damage.

With exquisite care the lid of the sarcophagus was pried loose and lifted off. The sarcophagus was empty! Empty—except for two silver bracelets set with butterflies of small bright stones.

Unknowingly, the young King Khufu had moved an empty sarcophagus down the deep shaft into the secret tomb. Probably the messenger who brought word to Khufu that the queen's burial chamber had been entered knew then that the mummy was missing. But in terror of the young Pharaoh's wild grief and rage if he were told the truth, the man had lied.

The mummy had been stolen for the great wealth of golden jewelry, amulets, and precious stones beneath the wrappings. Then, robbed of its treasure, the queen's mummy doubtless had been destroyed.

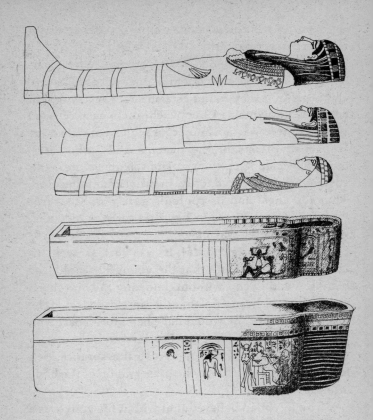

This diagram-drawing demonstrates the nesting of the mummy board and the coffin proper within the outer sarcophagus.

For the archeologists the empty sarcophagus was a bitter disappointment.

The blow was somewhat softened when they opened a sealed compartment in one wall of the burial chamber. In it they found an alabaster chest with four sections, known as a Canopic chest. In each of these sections there was a Canopic jar which contained the embalmed organs of the queen's body—the intestines, liver, stomach, lungs. The scientists knew this custom was practiced only in true mummification. Thus the chest and its contents gave proof that true mummification existed in Egypt as early as 2500 B.C., when Hetepheres was queen.

But poor King Khufu! It was just as well his informant had lied and that the young Pharaoh lived his life, and died, without knowing his mother's mummy had been stolen and destroyed. Had he known the truth, he would have been torn apart with grief and hopeless despair. For he—and all ancient Egyptians—believed that the greatest assurance for a life in the next world was the preservation of the body after death.

The Egyptian believed that within his body was a kind of spiritual "twin" called *ka,* a force that gave him life. Every person was born with his ka, and it dwelt within him as long as he lived. When he died, his ka left his body. But if his body was preserved, his ka would return to it so that he could live again.

But just in case something should happen to his

body, other precautions needed to be taken. Statues of the person, ka figures, were placed in the tomb. Drawings of him were on the tomb walls. His name was written on objects in the tomb so that his identity would never be lost.

However, these were substitutes. Ideally, his earthly body must continue to "live" in the tomb, protected and preserved in as lifelike a condition as possible. This was the reason for mummification.

Wrapping a corpse in bandages was not strange to the Egyptians. Bandaging the dead was deeply rooted in their religion. It was the miracle story of their great god Osiris and his life after death.

A beloved king on earth, Osiris had been murdered by his brother, Set. Set tore the body into fourteen pieces and scattered them along the Nile. Osiris' grief-stricken wife, Isis, after great tribulation, recovered all the pieces of her husband's body and put them back together with bindings of linen cloth. Calling on a netherworld god, Anubis, for help—and using powerful charms—Isis breathed life back into Osiris.

He could not return to earth as a man. But triumphantly Osiris entered the other world as its ruler and became the powerful god of the dead. Anubis became the god of preserving the body for the afterlife. And Isis became the protectress of the dead.

After her husband's death, Isis gave birth to a son, named Horus. On reaching manhood, Horus swore to avenge his father's murder, and engaged his uncle Set in a long and fearful battle. In the end Horus was victorious. But not before Set had plucked out the young man's left eye.

With the wicked Set destroyed and banished, Horus became a beloved god, protector of mankind. And his plucked eye became a potent symbol which would enable the deceased to see again. Depicted as a falcon's eye, drawings of "the Eye of Horus" and

Depicted as a falcon's eye, the drawing of "the Eye of Horus" became a powerful charm. The strong vertical line in the symbolic eye came to represent the tears of the god Horus.

amulets, or charms, made in its image were powerful and necessary symbols used in the rites of mummification.

If bandaging the corpse was not strange to the Egyptian, neither was the possibility of lifelike preservation of the body after death. In the hot, dry atmosphere of their sunlit land everything lasted. Even the thin papyrus the Egyptians wrote on endured. So why not man?

And digging into the sunbaked, sterile sand, the early Egyptians must often have come upon bodies well preserved by nature in their dry desert graves.

They knew bodies could remain whole and lifelike long after death. They had seen them.

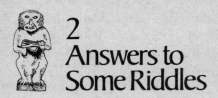

2
Answers to
Some Riddles

In our modern world we know three ways in which a body may be treated to preserve it.

Two of these methods were unknown in ancient Egypt but are used today.

One is by refrigeration, or placing the body in cold storage. This is impractical except on a small, temporary scale. It is used in police morgues, for example, where bodies must be held for examination or identification.

The second modern method is by injecting the body with fluids that are absorbed slowly and have qualities that aid in the preservation of tissue. We call this embalming. Even if the Egyptians had known this method, it would not have suited their purpose as it is effective for only a limited length of time, and the Egyptians believed that for a person to survive in the afterlife, the body must be preserved forever.

The third method is by thoroughly drying out the body—known as desiccation—and then treating the body so it will stay dry. This was the method devised by the people of ancient Egypt and used in creating mummies.

This method of desiccation must not have been easy, since the human body is 75 percent water. But so obsessed were the Egyptians with the preservation of the body after death, they managed to achieve it.

How it was done is not a mystery to us anymore, although almost two thousand years have elapsed since the Egyptians last made a mummy. Mummification stopped with the dawn of the Christian Era, when the people of Egypt were converted to Christianity. As Christians, and later as Muslims, they no longer believed that preservation of one's earthly body was necessary for life in the next world. The need for mummification ended.

But before they were converted to Christianity, they had practiced it for about twenty-five centuries. During all those ages thousands and thousands of priests, servants, workers were involved in the making of mummies and knew how it was done.

Yet, today, there exists one—and only one—eyewitness account by a man who actually saw mummies being made in ancient Egypt. He was a Greek, the scholar Herodotus, who went to Egypt as a visitor in the year 484 B.C.

There was never a more enthusiastic tourist than Herodotus. He made copious notes on everything he saw. Unfortunately, sometimes an Egyptian catching his enthusiasm would tell Herodotus an interesting but quite fanciful yarn, which he believed. So not all his stories about Egypt are true.

But his observations on mummy-making were firsthand. He wrote down what he saw and for many centuries his account was considered accurate and valid. For the most part, it was.

However, there was one point—the most important part of the mummification process—in which either Herodotus erred or a mistake was made in translation. This had to do with the drying out of the body, the desiccation process. According to Herodotus, this was done by soaking the body in an aqueous *solution* of a chemical known as natron, a sodium carbonate in crystalline form, before the wrapping began.

For centuries no one questioned this. Everyone writing on the art of mummification followed Herodotus and described the desiccation process as one of soaking the body over a long period of days in a natron solution.

Then, late in the nineteenth century, there began a great awakening of interest in ancient Egypt, especially in England. A few scholars dared to question Herodotus' account of the soaking process. They asked: If you have an object that is 75 percent water, do you place it in a natron solution to dry it out? While it might be possible to desiccate a body eventually by soaking it in a solution, surely it would be easier and more practical to do it with a dry chemical.

One of these men, an English scientist, Alfred Lucas, conducted an experiment in his laboratory with chickens. He plucked the birds and eviscerated them. One group he put to soak in a natron solution. The second group he completely covered with dry natron.

Within a few days the ones in solution began to give off a strong odor. Not so the ones in dry natron.

After forty days Lucas took them out. The ones in natron solution were bleached white. They were still plump and the skin looked intact. But they certainly were not dried out. He tried to handle them. It was impossible. The birds were pulpy and soft. The skin rubbed off. They fell apart.

The ones in dry natron were emaciated, dry, practically free from odor. Their skins were intact. They were easy to handle.

The experiment convinced Lucas that what he had thought all along was true—a body placed in a water solution would not dry out, not even in the arid, sun-hot land of Egypt. Dry natron was used.

Students of ancient Greece and its language dug back into the writings of Herodotus and theorized that a key word had been misconstrued in his writings on mummies. The key word was Ταριχεύουσι. This word could mean preserving by drying out, as fish were often dried out to be kept. Or this word could mean preserving by placing in a brine, or pickling, solution. The latter interpretation had been given to the word. And so for hundreds of years this is the way Herodotus' account was read and translated.

Today it is generally agreed that the desiccation was done with dry natron and that Herodotus was not inaccurate but misunderstood.

Meantime, the interest in ancient Egypt grew by leaps and bounds. Serious archeologists, as well as self-styled Egyptologists, traveled from Europe and the United States to the land of the Nile, excavating ancient sites, exploring the tombs and the temples.

Gradually more and more information on mummification and its rites was added to the account Herodotus left us. Some of the knowledge was gleaned from the drawings and writings on tomb and temple walls. Some was learned from objects found in the tombs: Canopic jars, unused linen and packets left by the ancient embalmers, their workshop tables, instruments they used.

A great deal was learned by scientists who carefully unwrapped mummies for study and analysis. Bit by bit the story of mummification was pieced together.

Despite all that has been learned, no one knows

exactly when the Egyptians first started wrapping their dead in bandages in an attempt to preserve the body. But a clue was discovered late in the last century.

A British archeologist, James Quibell, was digging in a flat desert area where an ancient cemetery had once been located. He knew this was a very old burial site, dating back to about 3000 B.C. One day he uncovered a box, squarish in shape—not oblong as later coffins were. Opening it, he found the body of a woman. It had been placed in the wooden box in a flexed position, that is, with the knees drawn up, which was the burial custom of that early period.

Quibell's excitement mounted when he saw that the body was completely wrapped in a complex series of bandages. He counted more than sixteen layers intact and judged that as many layers had probably been destroyed. Each leg was bandaged separately and the body was carefully wrapped. Between the bandages and the bones was a mass of corroded linen, which he took as evidence that some chemical had been applied to her body to preserve it. Quibell knew, then, that attempts at mummification had been made as early as 3000 B.C.—the 1st Dynasty in Egypt.

Alas, these early attempts had not succeeded in accomplishing the Egyptian's chief aims of mummification: one, to preserve the living form of the person who had died, and two, to preserve the body tissues. The woman Quibell had found, in spite of the bandaging, was not a successful mummy. She could not have been recognized or identified, and no tissue had survived. All that remained was the fine bone structure of her skull—the teeth still even and strong, proving that she was a young woman—and her body skeleton.

But the ancient embalmers were learning.

A few years after Quibell's discovery another British Egyptologist, Sir William M. Flinders Petrie, was excavating along the Nile, in the desert of Medûm, when he came upon an oblong coffin he dated around 2500 B.C., or the 4th Dynasty.

The mummy it contained, swathed in quantities of linen bandages, filled Petrie with amazement. The outer wrappings had been soaked with resin and then molded carefully into shape, so that every feature of the face and body was reproduced in the wrappings. This was a man who had died more than four thousand years ago. But, so beautifully molded were the wrappings, one who had known him in life would have recognized his wrapped mummy.

Petrie's mummy is the oldest one ever found that succeeded in preserving, outwardly, the living form and identity of the person who had died.

Yet, interesting as he was, the mummy of Medûm was not a successful mummy either. While the wrappings were lifelike, the mummy inside had not been preserved.

But from these early beginnings the Egyptians were to go on to become the greatest masters of embalming the world has ever known.

How did the Egyptians do it?

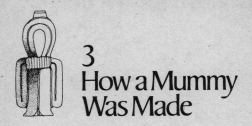

3
How a Mummy Was Made

The man is dead!

The high-pitched screams of the grieving women told the neighbors that the man had died. They knew him as a man of consequence, a good man, well-liked, a trusted official in their small city on the Nile.

They knew him as a man who enjoyed his family, his comfortable home, the walled garden with its flowers and reflecting pool. His life had been happy, as was theirs.

The neighbors now left their houses, their gardens, and courtyards to stand in their doorways or along the path of the hot, dusty street. The sun burned down from the cloudless Egyptian sky, and although it was not yet noon, the heat was almost unbearable. But the neighbors stood, waiting for the women of the dead man's household to appear.

They came—his wife, his young daughters, his

The procession of wailing women adapted from a wall painting in the tomb of the vizier, Rekmire of the 18th Dynasty also shows a portion of the funeral texts which were interwoven with the scenes.

old mother, his sisters. Their breasts were bared, their dresses belted tightly around their waists. As they cried out their grief, they scooped up dust, putting it on their heads, smudging it on their faces. Soon, damp with heat, their faces wet with tears, the dust became muddy smears, matting their hair, staining their skin.

Beating their breasts, they wandered through the streets of the city calling out the name of the dead for all to hear.

The men relatives followed the women. They, too, were bared to the waist and beat their chests with their fists to show their grief.

Later in the day they all returned to the house of the dead and composed themselves for another procession. This time, with the body on a litter, accompanied by priests, they followed it to the embalmer's workshop, where the body would be prepared for mummification.

It would take about ten weeks to create the mummy. During that period the family would remain, as much as possible, in their home, in seclusion, chanting dirges and mourning their loss.

The place where the body was taken for mummification was a large tent. Sometimes the embalmers' workshops were in permanent buildings. But in this country of heat and sun and almost no rain, tents were practical. They could be moved easily when necessary, and were more comfortable for the

HAIL, O YE WHO MAKE PERFECT
SOULS TO ENTER INTO THE HOUSE
OF OSIRIS; MAKE YE THE WELL
INSTRUCTED SOUL OF THE OSIRIS,
THE SCRIBE ANI WHOSE WORD IS
TRUE, TO ENTER IN AND TO BE
WITH YOU IN THE HOUSE OF OSIRIS.
LET HIM HEAR EVEN AS YE HEAR;
LET HIM HAVE SIGHT EVEN AS YE
HAVE SIGHT; LET HIM STAND UP
EVEN AS YE STAND UP; LET HIM
TAKE HIS SEAT EVEN AS YE TAKE
YOUR SEATS. . . .

embalmers to work in than the walled and confined space of a building.

The tent had cooled off during the night, and when the priests and workers gathered to begin their job, the air was pleasant.

The body, freshly bathed, was laid out on a long, narrow table, high enough so that those administering to the body need not bend over.

Beneath the table stood four stone jars, each about a foot high. These were the Canopic jars and later they would hold the embalmed larger organs of the man's body: the intestines, liver, stomach, lungs. The lid of each jar was topped with a figure carved of stone: one the head of a man, one a dog's head, one the head of a jackal, and one the head of a hawk.

The priest who was in charge of the embalming represented the god Anubis, who presided over mummification and was the guardian of the tombs. Since this god had the body of a man and the head of a jackal, this one priest wore a head mask of a jackal.

The priests were all freshly shaven; their heads, their faces—even their bodies beneath the fine, crisp linen robes—had been shaved to remove all hair. Led by the priest in the jackal mask, they intoned chants that announced the start of the work and the ritual.

The first actual step toward mummification was about to begin. This was the removal of the brain.

A specialist, highly skilled in his work, approached the head of the corpse. In his hand he held a long, slender hooklike instrument. Deftly he pushed this up one nostril, and working in a circular movement, he broke through the ethmoid bone, up into the cavity of the brain.

Withdrawing the hooklike instrument, he chose another. This one was a narrow, spirally twisted rod that had a small spoonlike tip. Pushing this up into the cranial cavity, he began, slowly, bit by bit, to draw out the brain through the nose, discarding each piece as he went along.

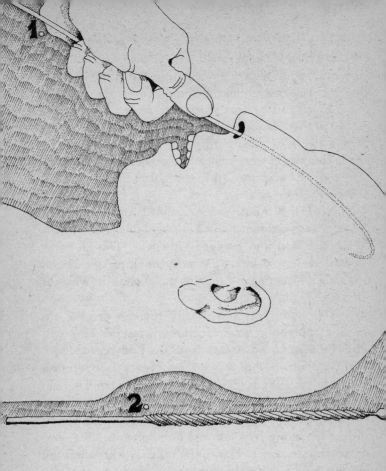

A diagram drawing shows two types of instruments possibly used in the removal of the brain. Instrument no. 1 is being inserted into the nostril, through the spongy bone and into the cranial cavity.

This was an operation of skill and patience. When at long last he was finished, satisfied that all of the brain had been removed from the cranial cavity, leaving it clean and clear, he prepared to leave. His job was done, and he was pleased to have done it well. Once in a while a clumsy operator crushed a bone or broke the nose, disfiguring the face forever. But he had completed the delicate operation leaving the strong bone structure, the well-shaped face, as it had been when he started.

Now the mouth was cleansed and in it were placed wads of linen soaked in sweet oils. The nostrils were cleansed and plugged with wax. The face was coated with a resinous paste. A small piece of linen was placed over each eye, and the eyelids drawn over them.

The body was now ready for the second important operation toward mummification. This was the removal of the viscera from the body cavity.

The man who was to perform this operation stood outside the tent, waiting to be called in. He held in his hand a fairly large, flat black stone, one edge of which was honed to razor sharpness. It was called an Ethiopian stone. His job was not a pleasant one, and gruesome to watch. Hence the other workers and the priests held him in abhorrence.

As he waited, the priest wearing the jackal mask approached the body, which had been turned slightly on its right side, exposing the left flank. The tent throbbed with the sound of the soft, rhythmic chantings of the priests.

The jackal head bent toward the body, and the masked priest dipped a small rush pen into a pot of ink, then drew on the left side of the body a spindle-shaped line about five inches long.

The priest stepped back and the man with the stone was called in. Following the line the priest had drawn, he cut, with great strength, through skin and flesh. Then, reaching through the incision, he severed and removed each organ: the stomach, liver, kidneys, lungs, intestines.

Only the heart was left in place. It was thought to be the seat of intelligence and feeling, and so must remain forever intact within the body.

The other vital organs would be wrapped in resin-soaked cloth and each placed in the proper Canopic jar. Their lids sealed on with wax, the jars would be set aside to await the day of burial.

His loathsome job finished, the man fled from the tent, followed by shouts of derision and contempt from all the others. He was considered unclean, and their angry outcries, the curses they called down on him, would rid the tent of his taint.

The priests, the embalmers, might pretend to despise him. But they all knew his job was an important one. Left in place, the internal organs would deteriorate rapidly, making the drying out of the body and successful mummification impossible.

The body cavity was cleansed with palm wine. The incision was pulled together, and a priest performed the ritual of placing on it a wax plate bearing the all-powerful symbol, the Eye of Horus. For a wealthier man the plate might have been of silver, or even of gold. But in any case, always, the Eye of Horus was depicted on it. Next, thin wires of gold

This scene depicts the first steps in mummification. Note the four Canopic jars beneath the embalming table and the Ethiopi-

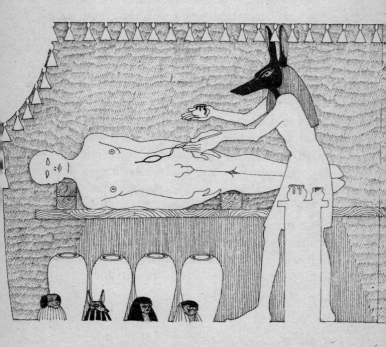

were fastened around each fingernail and toenail to keep them in place. And once again the corpse was bathed.

The body was now ready to be dried out.

The powder called natron came from the Libyan Desert. It was known to be a great drying agent and had cleansing and purification powers as well. Laid

an stone knife in the hand of the man waiting to perform the eviscration.

out on a fresh, clean mat woven of plant fibers, the body was covered with natron. In the hot, dry atmosphere, with the heat of the sun to help, day after day the drying-out process in the natron went on.

The day came when the body was wholly dry—the skin stretched on the firm frame of bone, the face thin but still the face of the man who had died.

The body was very light when the men lifted it onto a high table. It was bathed once more. It was anointed with ointments and rubbed with sweet-smelling spices and herbs.

Priests now poured out libations—liquid that symbolically restored moisture to the body. They lighted incense, which they burned—also symbolically—to restore the body's warmth and odor.

The body was ready to be wrapped.

About 150 yards of linen cloth had been prepared, torn into strips of varying widths. On some of the bandages the man's name was written. Thus his identity would be preserved. On some there were figures of the gods and on others were religious writings and words of magic. All of these would give the man help and power when he reached the other world.

The bandaging was intricate, and those doing the work were highly skilled. But only the priests knew where the magical bandages, with their words of power, should be placed. Only the priests knew the words to be chanted when the man's ring was placed

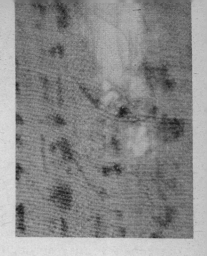

on his finger, the gold earrings hung in his ears. Only the priests could direct where, amongst the bandages, the amulets should be hidden to protect the deceased on his journey into the next world.

So as the bandaging began, and as it went on, there were frequent interludes when the wrapping ceased while the priests, with great ceremony, intoned their words of wisdom and chanted religious formulas.

Thus the wrapping, with its wealth of religious significance, took some time. And seventy days elapsed between the day of the man's death and the day when the wrapping was finished. On that day the mummy was taken back to the house of mourning where the man had died.

From the house the final procession set forth. The mummy, in its elaborately painted mummiform coffin, lay upon a lion-headed bier which was placed on a sledge drawn by men and oxen. Walking before the sledge, on each side, were two women who impersonated the goddess Isis and her sister goddess, Nephthys, guardians of the dead. Behind the bier came another sledge, drawn by men. On this was a chest that held the four Canopic jars.

The women mourners followed, wailing in grief, their hair disheveled. Then came the men mourners, beating their breasts in sorrow. Behind the mourners were the servants, carrying the objects the dead man would need for living in the other world: chests filled with clothes, toilet articles, jars of salves and unguents, and some of his favorite possessions. Others bore the funerary furniture: a bed, a chair, small stools.

When the procession reached the entrance of the tomb, the mummy was taken from its bier and set in a standing position on a mound of sand, facing the mourners.

While the mourners watched and waited, the priests began the long, complicated series of rituals that would assure the man success on his long journey into the next world. Small vessels of burning incense were waved, rites of purification, lustration, were performed. The ceremonies went on and on. Finally

The *adze*, an everyday carpenter's tool used to hew wood, became for the ancient Egyptians in its model size, a potent amulet in the "Opening of the Mouth" ceremony. Scene above the mummy enacts this ceremony.

came the most complex and important rite of all, known as the Opening of the Mouth.

One priest, holding a miniature *adze* that possessed special mystical powers, approached the mummy. To the chanting of religious formulas, he touched the mummy's head: the eyes, to open them so the man could see; the ears, so he could hear; the mouth, so he could speak; the jaws, so he could eat.

He could now live in the other world as he had on earth. He would need the contents of his carved chests, the furniture placed in his tomb, the food and drink that would be provided for him.

Even as the coffined body, sealed in its sarcophagus, was being placed in its tomb, the man's journey into the next world had begun.

The mourners, weary from their hot and dusty procession to the tomb and the long-lasting ceremonies that followed, were now ready to enjoy the great feast that had been prepared for them. Knowing that the dead man was on his way to a second happy life that would never end, they partook of a joyous banquet. The foods were the finest, the wines and beer plentiful. There were entertainers and musicians, and guests sang songs in praise of the man just buried.

The mourning was over.

4
The Tombs: Their Builders and Plunderers

The man whose mummy was just buried was not a nobleman, nor even a man of vast wealth. So his tomb was relatively modest. It consisted of two rooms.

One room—the burial chamber—was cut deep in the rock, at the end of a shaft. Here the mummy in its coffin was placed, along with objects the deceased would need for his life in the next world.

Although the jewelry and amulets in his wrappings, the objects in his burial chamber, were not to be compared with the treasures of a Pharaoh, thieves might be tempted. So every precaution was taken to protect the mummy and thwart the robbing of his tomb.

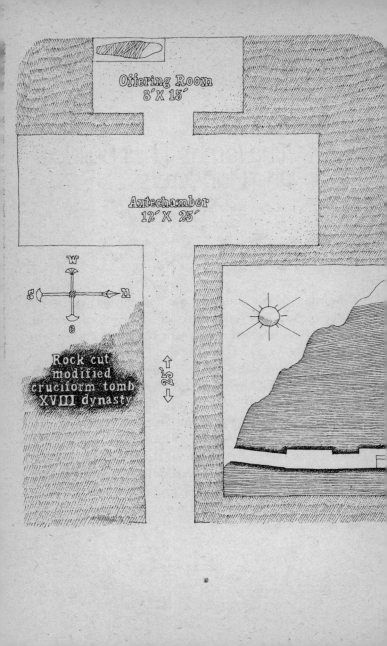

Offering Room
8' X 15'

Antechamber
12' X 25'

W
S   N
E

Rock cut
modified
cruciform tomb
XVIII dynasty

The burial chamber door was sealed and a block of stone pushed in front of it. The shaft leading down to it was filled with sand and rock.

The second room, a small room, was above this, near the tomb's entrance. Here food and drink would be placed regularly, for it was believed the dead person needed to eat and drink in the second world as he had on earth.

On one wall of this room was a false door where the soul of the deceased appeared to accept offerings of food and drink left for him. On another wall was a small slit. Behind this stood a statue of the dead man—his ka figure.

Long before he died, the man had done what every Egyptian who could afford to did—he contracted with a ka priest to keep food supplied in his tomb. The food, wine, and beer would be similar to that he had enjoyed at his own table when he lived.

For a poorer man the offerings of food and drink would be very simple: bread, a few vegetables, and perhaps a piece of fish occasionally. But for the wealthy the food replenished regularly in the tomb was a sumptuous feast: breads and cakes, a rich variety of roast meats, poultry, game birds, vegetables and fruits, different kinds of beer and fine wines.

In the early days of Egypt's history, when it was deemed safe to keep the mummy in a chamber near the entrance of the tomb, the food was placed right in the burial chamber. But as grave robbers became bolder and the fear of thieves despoiling the mummy grew, burial chambers were hidden deeper and deeper within the tombs. Then it became necessary to add an extra room, close to the entrance, where food could be offered.

The tombs became more and more complicated. They also grew in size and magnificence, especially the tombs the Pharaohs built for themselves. The most spectacular and famous of the Egyptian tombs is the Great Pyramid of Giza, built by the Pharaoh Khufu, who is also known by his Greek name, Cheops.

Many pyramid tombs were built along the Nile by ancient Pharaohs—more than seventy we know—and many of great size. But Khufu's was by far the largest.

Khufu ruled about 4,500 years ago, in the beginning of the 4th Dynasty. Yet today, when the most complicated and sophisticated engineering feats are taken for granted, we marvel at this incredible structure and wonder that it was ever achieved.

It still stands as the largest stone structure in the world. Its base covers thirteen acres. Two million three hundred thousand blocks of stone were used, each weighing from two to thirteen tons.

It took 100,000 men more than twenty years to build Khufu's pyramid. And the toll of human lives must have been terrible. They worked in relentless heat, dirt, wind, and sand. The wheel had not been invented then, nor had the pulley.

Men cut the stone—nearly ten billion pounds—from quarries east of Giza, across the Nile. They loaded the enormous stones on barges, and men harnessed with ropes pulled the sledges to the river. When the waters rose and the flats were flooded, they

The Great Pyramid at Giza was built to house and protect Khufu's mummy. Foreground shows the remains of the Valley Temple of Khafra. In mid-distance is the famous Sphinx of Giza. Courtesy of Hirmer Verlag, München.

moved the stones onto huge rafts and floated them across the wide valley. At the base of the hill on which the pyramid was being built, an immense ramp was constructed. Up this incline the stones were hauled. Then came the formidable task of lifting them into position. With the use of ropes and small graveled ramps, gangs of men managed to push and haul and lift them into place.

These thousands of men lived where they worked. Hence a small city had to be built to house them and to provide for all their needs. It is thought that they were allowed to go home, in shifts, to sow their crops. But on the whole, for twenty years or more this tremendous amount of manpower was spent on building a tomb in the desert.

The cost of building even a small pyramid was enormous. The price of the Great Pyramid of Giza must have been astronomical.

Was Khufu ever buried in his magnificent tomb? No one knows. His burial chamber was empty when an entrance into the pyramid was found in modern times. What we can be sure of was that he never forgot that the tomb of his mother, Queen Hetepheres, had been entered, making it necessary for him to move her sarcophagus to a secret hiding place.

So, even though he had his burial chamber built deep within the great stone pyramid, roofed with gigantic granite slabs, and equipped with a complicated device for plugging the passage leading to it once the mummy was placed inside, he still may have feared for the safety of his mummy there. For his pyramid tomb, by the time it was finished, had attracted an enormous amount of attention.

Every one of the pyramids, scattered for miles along the Nile, had elaborate devices for protecting the mummy in its burial chamber. There were hidden entrances and a network of passages meant to baffle the tomb robbers. There were false sepulchers to lure the thieves in wrong directions. There were trap doors blocked with stones of incredible size and weight.

Some burial chambers within the pyramids had no doors at all. Instead a hole, through which the sarcophagus could be lowered, was cut in the roof of the chamber. The hole was then blocked with a great slab of stone. These roof blocks were often colossal. The doorless chamber of the Pyramid of Hawara had a roof block that weighed forty-five tons, and could be reached only by descending a steep, many-angled corridor and negotiating three trapdoors, barricaded with great stone doorblocks.

But all these devices were in vain. Every one of the pyramids, and all their burial chambers, were entered and robbed. Not one escaped.

The pyramids were magnificent monuments. But they failed as tombs. They did not protect the mummies of their builders; they failed to assure the Pharaohs a life after death.

So the Pharaohs who followed turned away from

these colossal aboveground monuments that dominated the landscape. They had their tombs hewn deep in the rock walls of cliffs.

Compared with the high, imposing pyramids reaching toward the sky, the rock cliff tombs, from the outside, were dull and uninviting. Often the entrance was just a narrow cut in the rock wall. But inside, many of these tombs were vast, magnificent in architecture, and lavishly decorated.

The tomb of a Pharaoh who had enjoyed a long and prosperous reign—such as Ramesses II— contained as many as twenty rooms, every wall covered with paintings. Even a lesser noble, a lord named Ameni, built himself a tomb of such grandeur that the entrance room alone, with its high, vaulted ceiling, is so large, a man standing in it is dwarfed by its size.

To hew these vast, complex tombs out of rock and lavishly decorate their many rooms required a large population of workmen and artists, just as the pyramids did. They too lived where they worked, in houses built near the site of the tomb. To fill their needs there had to be a community of workers and tradespeople: butchers, weavers, water carriers, brewers to make their beer, bakers to bake their bread.

Money was not used in Egypt then, and the tombs workmen and artisans were paid in rations of food and clothing. In good times the pay was adequate. But if times were poor—or the officials responsible for paying them were greedy and dishonest—their lot could be hard indeed.

Sometimes things got so bad, the workmen went on strike. A record of one such strike tells of the men leaving their jobs and sending a delegation to the Pharaoh's representative, pleading: ". . . We have come urged by hunger, urged by thirst; we have no linen, no oil, no fish, no vegetables. . . . Inform our pharaoh, our lord, so that he may obtain for us the means of life. . . ."

And even in good times building the tombs must have been brutally hard work, much of it done under difficult, almost impossible, conditions. Underground in the airless chambers and deep shafts their only light came from flickering ragwicks burning in small bowls of oil. With this dim light, and using primitive tools, these men managed somehow to achieve the elegant, multichambered tombs with their labyrinths of stairways and corridors that led down, hundreds of feet down, to the burial chambers below.

But no matter how deep and intricately the tombs were dug, how far down the burial chambers were placed, the thieves got in.

Only one mummy of a Pharaoh unmolested by grave robbers has been found. He was a boy-king who came to the throne probably at the age of

A craftsman of ancient Egypt sculpts a hunting dog into the stone wall of an Old Kingdom tomb. On the ground lie four other carving tools. Egyptologists believe the tomb decorators used natural light aided by reflecting devices whenever possible. But many deep chambers must have been lighted by oil lamps.

ten. He was eighteen when he died. Unimportant in his own time, today he is the most famous Pharaoh of all.

The young king's name was Tutankhamen. His teen-age queen was named Ankhesenamun. Little is known of them, but they married very young, perhaps when eleven or twelve years old.

His reign was short and his tomb was small and unpretentious. It consisted of three modest white-washed rooms and a burial chamber so small there was barely space in it for his sarcophagus.

But the richness and beauty of the objects found in this minor king's tomb give us a dazzling sample of the treasure, the fortune in jewels and gold, that was buried with the greater Pharaohs.

Had his tomb been emptied of its treasure by thieves, or had it remained hidden beneath its rubble, Tutankhamen's name would be almost unknown to-day.

But fortunately the treasure lay hidden. And thanks to the determination of an English archeologist, Howard Carter, the tomb was discovered.

For years Carter had been excavating in a bleak and barren area known as the Valley of the Kings. Sun-scorched by the unbearable heat in summer, hot and arid the year through, the valley is a desolate place of rocks and cliffs and mounds of sand. Cut into the faces of the rocks and cliffs are many openings. These are entrances leading to subterranean tombs built in the day of the ancient Pharaohs. The valley got its name from the fact that so many kings and their nobles were buried there.

Naturally the valley, honeycombed with royal tombs, attracted archeologists. But long before the archeologists, it had attracted tomb robbers. So, while many men had excavated there before Carter, all the tombs had been plundered. Every mummy had been damaged and robbed.

Yet Carter believed that one small, unimportant king, named Tutankhamen, had been buried somewhere in the valley, and that his tomb had not been found.

Other archeologists disagreed with him; they argued that the tomb and all its contents had been plundered and destroyed long ago. Every inch of the valley had been dug out, they said. There was nothing more to find.

For five years Carter doggedly excavated, searching for the tomb. He had no money of his own. But he had a benefactor: Lord Carnarvon, an Englishman of wealth who was interested in Egyptian archeological finds.

At long last Lord Carnarvon, too, decided there was nothing more to find in the valley. He asked Carter to come to visit him at his home in England, Highclere Castle, and there reluctantly told Carter he was withdrawing his support.

One night, while still in England, Carter was

poring over maps of the valley and pinpointed a small triangular space they had not explored. It was a barren area covered with loose rocks, sand, and rubble. Small, unpromising, and situated at the base of the great tomb of Ramesses VI, it was an unlikely spot for another Pharaoh's tomb. Diggers, quite reasonably, had passed it by.

The site of Tutankhamen's tomb in the Valley of the Kings. The square hole above the tent is the entrance to the tomb. The larger rectangular opening to the right is the entrance to the tomb of Ramesses VI. Photo by Harry Burton, The Metropolitan Museum of Art.

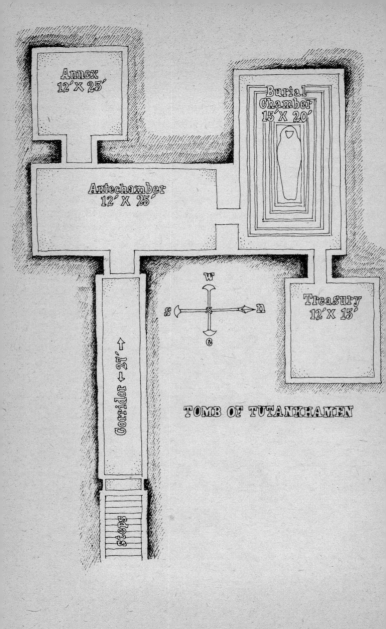

TOMB OF TUTANKHAMEN

But Carter pointed it out to Carnarvon and begged him to finance just one more season of digging. Carnarvon agreed.

Carter returned to Egypt and on November 1, 1922, he and his crew began clearing the wedge of land. Three days later they discovered a step cut in the rock beneath an ancient workman's hut they had uncovered. A little more clearing revealed this to be the first of sixteen steps leading down into more rock. At the foot of the stairs there was a door, blocked with piles of stone.

After the workmen removed the stones, Carter was excited to see impressions of seals pressed into the door, indicating a royal burial. He now knew, at long last, that he had found a royal tomb.

Carter later said, "I needed all my self-control to keep from breaking down the doorway . . . then and there."

To open it at once he felt would not be fair to his benefactor, Lord Carnarvon, who was still in England. He went to the nearby city of Luxor and cabled Carnarvon:

> . . . MADE WONDERFUL DISCOVERY IN VALLEY.
> A MAGNIFICENT TOMB WITH SEALS INTACT.
> RE-COVERED SAME FOR YOUR ARRIVAL.
> CONGRATULATIONS.

So the workmen blocked the door once more and

filled in the stairway with rubble. Carter placed guards on watch and, half mad with impatience, awaited Carnarvon's arrival.

Lord Carnarvon reached Luxor on November 23. By the following day the rubble and stones were again cleared, and the two men, accompanied by a few aides, went down to examine the door. To their bitter disappointment they saw now that Carter was mistaken. The seals had been broken, and resealed. They removed the door and entered a narrow, empty corridor. At the end of the corridor was another door, the door to the tomb itself. To the men's despair they saw that this door, too, had been forced open and resealed.

Graverobbers had been there before them! Would they find just another empty tomb?

With trembling hands Carter made a small opening in the upper left-hand corner of the door. He held a lighted candle to the opening and peered in.

The candle sputtered. For a moment he saw nothing. Then, in Carter's own words:

> As my eyes grew accustomed to the light, details of the room within emerged slowly from the mist, strange animals, statues, and gold—everywhere the glint of gold. For the moment—an eternity it must have seemed to the others standing by—I was struck dumb with amazement. And when Lord Carnar-

von, unable to stand the suspense any longer, inquired anxiously, "Can you see anything?" it was all I could do to get out the words, "Yes. Wonderful things."

Carter handed Lord Carnarvon the candle.

5 The Golden Mummy of the Boy-King

When the door was removed, the men saw that all was in disorder. Thieves had been there—probably shortly after the young king's burial.

Apparently they had been surprised and scared off by guards or priests before they did much harm. But they had left their greasy fingerprints where they had emptied valuable oils from alabaster vases. There was a footprint on the floor. In their haste to flee when discovered, they had left behind waterskins partly filled with oil. One thief had dropped a number of gold rings he had wrapped in a linen cloth. Two gold struts were broken from a golden chair. A small statue, probably of gold, was missing, ripped from its base.

But very little had been taken, very little damage done.

Carter, Carnarvon, and their aides had entered a virtually intact tomb of a Pharaoh—the only one that had ever been found.

This room, which Carter called the antechamber, was the largest of the four rooms they were to find in the tomb. Even so, it was small by comparison with chambers in other royal tombs—25 feet long and just 12 feet wide. The whitewashed walls were plain and unadorned.

But this room, and two smaller "storage rooms" they entered later, were crammed with treasures. The wealth that had been buried with this boy-king for more than three thousand years dazzled the eyes and boggled the mind. Objects of gold and silver, turquoise, carnelian, lapis lazuli, carved ivory and alabaster . . .

There was the young Pharaoh's gold and silver throne, set with semiprecious stones; gilded couches with carved animal bed-heads. There was a golden shrine that held the alabaster Canopic chest. Within the chest, in each of the four compartments, lay a small coffin, exquisitely wrought of gold and cloisonné, containing the embalmed organs from the body of the king.

There was a whole fleet of model boats—ready to fill the Pharaoh's every sailing wish—including one of alabaster, inlaid with gold and precious stones.

The gold-sheathed ceremonial chariots he had used on earth were there—dismantled because they were too large to be drawn through the narrow corridor into the small room.

To serve him in his second life, there were servants: more than a hundred statuettes of men and women, called *ushabti.* And with them were almost

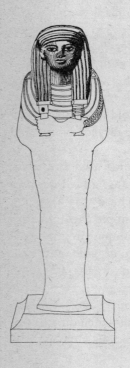

This wooden servant-statue known as *shawabti* or *ushabti* carried out his master's bidding in the nether-world. Actual size of figure was approximately 12 inches high.

two thousand tools and implements they would use in their king's service.

In magnificently decorated chests were his royal robes, some covered with gold sequins, others decorated with pure gold rosettes; his sandals worked with gold.

These and hundreds of other things were in the tomb, ready for his use in the next world.

Among the many objects of beauty, a few cast some light on the shadowy figure of the young king, Tutankhamen. His marriage to the girl-queen is pictured as a happy one. Scenes from their daily life are exquisitely drawn on the side panels of a gold shrine or chest. The queen is shown bringing flowers and unguents to her king; solicitously she fastens a gold collar around his neck; the king pours perfumed oil into the queen's small, cupped hand; and in yet another panel they are shown hunting together, the king with bow drawn, the queen handing him an arrow.

Again we see them happily pictured on the back of the king's gold and silver throne, in a work of glowing colors and semiprecious stones. The king, seated, is turned toward his wife, who is leaning down touching his shoulder, possibly anointing it with oil. And their extreme youth when married is evident in a painting on ivory, the childlike pair in a garden, the queen holding two lotus blooms, the king's hand outstretched to accept them. It is a love scene, the flowers entwined with mandrake, the fruit of love.

The tomb tells us that the young king was a great hunter. Hundreds of bows and arrows were placed there for his use. There are pictures showing him hunting large game and small animals, wild ducks and other fowl. But he was fond of animals, too; he had a pet lion.

We know he enjoyed a popular chesslike game called *senet.* A number of handsome sets of varying sizes, made of ebony and ivory and inlaid with gold, were found in the tomb, their pieces, or "men," intact, ready for a game.

He played the trumpet. Two were buried with him. One of solid silver was placed in the shrine that held his sarcophagus.

But their marriage had seen sad times, too. In a wooden box standing near the king's Canopic chest were found two small coffins of wood, beautifully decorated. Inside each wooden coffin was another coffin, of solid gold. In each golden coffin was the mummy of a baby born prematurely.

Did they belong to Tutankhamen and his young queen? Probably so. We know he left no heirs.

When Carter first entered the antechamber, piled high with treasures, his eyes were caught by two life-size statues of the king. Handsome in black and gold, holding scepters of gold, they stood at each side of a sealed door. Carter guessed at once that they guarded the royal sarcophagus. Behind that door he should find the mummy of the Pharaoh Tutank-hamen.

If the sarcophagus had not been broken into, if the mummy remained intact, this would be the most important archeological find in all Egypt and one of the most important in all the world. This would be the first royal mummy ever found in its original coffins, its wrappings undisturbed.

As anxious as Carter and Lord Carnarvon were to see the sarcophagus, almost three months passed between discovery of the tomb and opening of the door to the burial chamber.

First they had to empty the antechamber. Every object in the room must be examined, cataloged, and photographed before it could be moved. Steps had to be taken, too, to preserve objects that might be harmed when exposed to outside air. For example, there were fragile objects that might disintegrate. Experts working with Carter hastened to preserve these in wax: the ostrich feathers of the king's fans, the wreaths of flowers still standing against the walls.

Finally, only the two black and gold statues of the king were left in place, guarding the door.

By now the discovery of the tomb had attracted world-wide attention. When he was finally ready to open the burial chamber, Carter had an invited audience seated on folding chairs in the emptied white-washed room. The room was charged with excitement.

Carter made a small opening in the top of the sealed door. Using a flashlight, he peered in. There, within a yard of the doorway, he was astonished to see a solid wall of gold. It stretched as far as he could see and seemed to block the entrance to the chamber.

When the door was removed, Carter and Lord Carnarvon squeezed into the narrow passage between the "wall" of gold and the walls of the burial chamber. They found it was not a wall of gold. It was a large gilt shrine, apparently built around the sarcophagus for protection. It practically filled the burial chamber. Almost 11 feet wide, more than 16 feet long, and 9 feet high, it nearly touched the ceiling. The space between it and the four walls of the room was a little more than 2 feet. That left a very narrow space for the men to move around in.

There were two wide doors to the shrine, which Carter removed. Inside was another gold shrine. Now Carter's excitement was intense! The seals on the doors had never been tampered with. For the first time since the days of ancient Egypt, men would soon see the intact sepulcher of an Egyptian king, his mummy in its coffins just as it was on the day of his burial.

Removing the doors of the second shrine, Carter found a third one. And nested inside that, a fourth.

As the men carefully removed each shrine, they found rich and beautiful objects: elaborate lamps of milky alabaster, staffs of gold and silver, painted alabaster jars with lids of carved figures, small chests inlaid with gold. Over one shrine hung a sheer cloth canopy sprinkled with bright gilded daisies.

The fourth, and last, golden shrine contained the magnificent red quartzite sarcophagus. At each corner, in high relief, was the figure of a goddess, her winged arms spread out protectingly.

When the sarcophagus was opened, Carter found three coffins, each shaped like a mummy. They nestled tightly, one within the other, so tightly that Carter could scarcely wedge his little finger between them.

Opening these coffins was to prove one of the toughest jobs in Carter's entire career. The task would take a tremendous amount of ingenuity and a long stretch of time. In addition to their being wedged tightly, libations which had been poured during the burial rites had hardened, so they were "glued" together. Carter's tedious and time-consuming problem was to open each coffin and lift it out without damaging it. He said later that throughout the ordeal his "nerves were at painful tension."

To make the job more difficult, the room in which he worked was always crowded with men watching him. This bothered Carter.

But he and all who watched were astonished by the beauty of the coffins. Each was a figure of the young king wearing the false beard and headdress of the Pharaohs. His hands, folded across his breast,

79

held the crook and flail, symbols of Egyptian royalty.

The first and second coffins were of gilded wood, inlaid with bits of gold and brilliant red and blue stones: carnelian and lapis lazuli.

The third coffin was of solid gold.

Carter and those with him gazed in awe. The rich

The gold mummiform coffin of Tutankhamen is the only example of its kind ever found. Courtesy of Hirmer Verlag, München.

beauty of the golden figure of the young Pharaoh was overwhelming.

The coffin was massive. More than 6 feet long, it contained 2,448 pounds of twenty-two-carat gold. But there was a delicacy in its elegance, the flowing lines of the goddesses etched in gold, the soft glow of stones set in graceful designs. Inside this coffin of gold was the mummy of the king.

Within the wrappings that enfolded him was found a whole treasury of ornaments: on his head the royal diadem of gold set with carnelian, lapis lazuli, and turquoise; collars and necklaces, golden girdles, amulets and pendants, pectorals—intricately wrought treasures of great beauty and exquisite workmanship. His slender hands were heavy with jewel-studded gold rings. And gold nail stalls were fitted on his fingers and toes.

Most wondrous of all was the portraitlike mask that had been placed on the bandaged face. Wrought of gold inlaid with gems, it covered the king's head and shoulders and extended down to the middle of his body. It was almost an exact likeness of the young king: the wide-open eyes luminous, the shining golden face noble and serene.

Tragically, Lord Carnarvon did not live to see the coffins opened and the young king's mummy revealed. Less than five months after the tomb was discovered, he was bitten by an insect in the Valley of the Kings. Blood poisoning set in and he died in a hospital in Cairo.

Some said, dramatically, that Carnarvon's death was due to "the Curse of the Pharaoh"—the revenge for the king's tomb being entered and the mummy unwrapped. Many believed this.

For years newspapers made a big thing of the curse when anyone connected with the tomb happened to die—from whatever cause. Meantime others pointed out that the surgeon who actually unwrapped the mummy, Dr. Douglas Derry, lived on for many years—well into his eighties. Surely if anybody had been cursed it would have been he. And Carter, the first man to enter the tomb, lived for eighteen years after he discovered it.

But old superstitions are hard to kill. And the curse of the Pharaoh lives on, down to the present.

When the fiftieth anniversary of the tomb's discovery was to be celebrated in 1972, England requested permission to borrow some of the tomb's finest objects from the museum in Cairo for a temporary exhibit in the British Museum. Many Egyptians violently opposed moving the treasures out of Egypt. The Minister of Culture of the Egyptian government, however, had the final say, and he allowed some of the treasures to be moved.

One week after the curator signed the papers permitting the treasures—for the first time—to leave Cairo, he dropped dead.

Once again people cried, "The Curse of the Pharaoh!"

Almost six years elapsed from the day the tomb was discovered by Carter until it was emptied and its treasures moved to the museum in Cairo.

No, not emptied. For the mummy of the young king was left in its simple whitewashed tomb, lying in the second coffin, resting in the handsome quartzite sarcophagus where it had been placed more than three thousand years before.

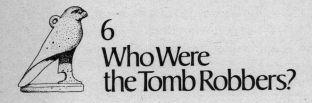

6
Who Were the Tomb Robbers?

The riches in the tomb of a wealthy man were not kept secret. They were paraded before the thousands who lined the hot, dusty path of the funeral procession. The jeweled chests, the golden furniture, statues of gold and silver, figures set with precious stones—all passed before the watching eyes.

Many of those watching were very poor— laborers who had sweated and struggled to help build the rich one's tomb; artisans who had toiled to fashion the furniture plated with gold. The gems pried loose from one small figure, the gold melted down from a single ornament, would fulfill all a family's needs. Even more important, they would provide for a man's own mummification and decent burial and his continued life in the next world.

The poor must have been sorely tempted.

Some of those watching were clever and wily. Among them were the professional thieves, experienced tomb robbers, making their plans as the procession passed by. Others were the corrupt and greedy, who would connive with the thieves and split the loot.

There was the coffinmaker who worked with the robbers. As he fashioned the coffin, he placed a small door in one end, then cleverly masked this addition. It was a simple matter for thieves breaking into the tomb to slide open the door and pull out the bejeweled mummy.

There was the sealer of the tomb who faithfully sealed the third, and last, door in the presence of the family. But the two inner doors he purposely left unprotected. Robbers, tunneling in, stripped the tomb bare at their convenience.

There were the guardians of the tombs, sometimes the priests themselves, who let the plunderers in and looked the other way in exchange for their share of the treasure.

There were the corrupt officials, bribed to give the thieves protection.

Where so much gold was involved, there was bound to be lust and greed. For gold was not easy to come by in ancient Egypt.

Some gold was mined in the granite mountains

that bordered the Red Sea. But most of Egypt's gold came from conquered peoples, extracted from them in the form of tribute. At one time Nubia, a conquered country that lay south of Egypt, was required to send 800 pounds of gold a year into the treasury of the Pharaoh. But even this amount did not go far when the gold coffin of one unimportant king, Tutankhamen, weighed three times that much.

Mining gold in that torrid, treeless desert country was not easy. When the great king Ramesses II, wanting more gold, sent a large caravan south into Nubia in an attempt to develop new mines, half the men died of thirst before they got there.

The tomb robbers knew an easier way to get gold. So even when robbing a tomb was punishable by death, even though the thief was doomed by his gods, the plundering continued, century after century.

A few of the robbers must have felt guilty desecrating the dead. For there are examples of the thief's trying to rewrap the mummy after robbing it; hurriedly putting it back together, leaving some bones out in his haste, pasting the bandages in place with a rough mixture of sand and resin.

Once in a great while the graverobbers were fooled and jewels were saved. There was a princess named Senebtisi, daughter of Aty, whose mummy was found with its beautiful pendants of gold and silver, jeweled rings, and a charm case of gilded filigree. It had not been robbed because she was a very tiny woman, placed in a small coffin, and the thieves apparently thought it was the coffin of a child, whose mummy would contain objects of little value.

It is ironic that what the kings and the wealthy could not achieve, the poor people did. The poor succeeded in keeping their mummies unmolested by robbers, safe in their tombs. These mummies, placed in communal tombs, the bodies often stacked one on top of another like so much cordwood, held nothing of value for the thieves. They were allowed to rest in peace, to continue their journey into the other world.

Not so the kings! Even in modern times, in this century, graverobbers have continued to molest the royal mummies. As late as 1901 thieves in the Valley of the Kings broke into the tomb of Amenophis II (who died about 1420 B.C.) and cut through the bandages in search of treasure. But they were more than three thousand years too late. Others like them—perhaps their ancestors—had been there long, long ago and stolen everything.

As recently as 1970 archeologists working in the Western Acropolis of Giza found the skeleton of a graverobber literally killed in the act. The men were excavating around a fallen limestone roofing slab when they came upon a sarcophagus, the lid of which had been pushed partly open. Alongside the sarcophagus was slumped a skeleton. One arm was stretched up to the lid of the sarcophagus and the bony hand was reaching inside, ready to search for loot.

At first the archeologists assumed he was a tomb robber from ancient times. Then they noted a half-rotted garment around the skeleton. It was a man's coat. In one pocket was a newspaper, still partly legible, dated 1944.

This twentieth-century tomb robber had been crushed to death at the scene of the crime when the heavy limestone roofing slab slipped.

It was also a band of graverobbers in modern times that solved a mystery for archeologists in Egypt. The mystery was what had happened to all the royal mummies of the great Pharaohs who had ruled Egypt over a period of about three hundred years—from the end of the 17th Dynasty into the 20th. Their original tombs, cut in the rock cliffs of Thebes, had been found, vast and empty.

Among them were some of Egypt's most famous Pharaohs: Amenophis I, Tuthmosis II and III, Seti I, Ramesses I, II, and III.

Since a whole line of kings was missing without a trace, archeologists guessed the bodies had been moved. They were correct. The bodies had been moved not long after the last of the missing Pharaohs, Ramesses III, was placed in his tomb in 1167 B.C.

Up until then the deeply cut cliff tombs in the

An artist's reconstruction of the physical appearance of
Ramesses II based upon the mummy.

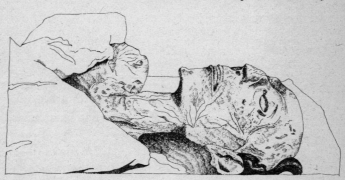

The mummy of King Ramesses II as it appeared shortly after its unwrapping.

Valley of the Kings were considered impregnable. And that was why the great Pharaohs had been buried there.

Nearby, on the Theban plains, were the tombs of lesser nobles. Occasionally one of these—easier to enter than the cliff tombs—had been robbed, but not often. The thief, if caught, was tortured and executed, and his ugly death was a powerful deterrent to others who might be tempted.

Then suddenly, around 1200 B.C., this changed. The Theban plains tombs were being robbed in shocking numbers. Finally a ring of thieves was caught. But instead of swift and terrible punishment being meted out, a high government official came to their defense.

Their protector was the mayor of Western Thebes, a man named Pawar. He was undoubtedly corrupt and in league with the tomb robbers. He maintained that a mistake had been made; the men were innocent. So powerful was his influence, the thieves were set free.

This example of official corruption and connivance greatly encouraged the robbing of tombs. The thieves now boldly moved from the plains into the cliff tombs of the Pharaohs. Immense and complex as these tombs were, they were looted. Burial chambers thought to be impregnable were entered, and their mummies, bandages ripped and cut, were robbed of their treasures. One great funerary temple was pillaged by its own tomb priests!

Finally the officials and high priests realized it was no longer possible to protect the royal mummies where they lay. They would have to be moved.

To find a safe and secret tomb for each of the

mummies was not possible. What was needed was a well-hidden chamber large enough to hold a number of the sarcophagi. This was found. Then they were faced with the formidable job of moving their dead.

First the high priests replaced the mummies' torn bandages or rebandaged them as best they could, for every mummy had been robbed. Then each mummy was labeled so that its identity would never be in doubt.

The herculean job of raising each sarcophagus from its deeply placed burial chamber was done, somehow, using only ropes and man power. After that came the task of transporting the sarcophagi—thirty of them—to their second tomb. Some were so heavy, it took more than a dozen men to lift one. And complicating the undertaking was the fact that it had to be done in secret, without attracting attention.

All the objects the thieves had left in the tombs were carried to the new resting place too. The thieves had stolen the gold funeral furniture, the shrines, the caskets of gold, chests inlaid with gold and gems. But the objects they spurned as being of little value—stone statues, tablets, scarabs, objects made of wood, papyri—these were moved with the mummies.

For three thousand years the mummies lay side by side in their new tomb, undisturbed, undiscovered.

Then one day in 1874 a young French Egyptologist, Gaston Maspero, living in Western Thebes, was amazed to learn that objects of Egyptian antiquity were appearing in antique markets. First there were a few small statues engraved with the name of a Pharaoh. Then there was a papyrus that belonged to a queen. And later, an ancient small wooden tablet. Inscriptions showed that all the pieces had belonged to royal persons who had lived in Thebes several thousand years ago.

Maspero, with the aid of detectives and others, began the tedious business of trying to find where these treasures of antiquity were coming from and who the thieves were. It was an almost impossible job. The hillsides in that desert land were, and still are, honeycombed with ancient tombs. Then, as now, the poorer people lived in them. The tombs were their homes.

Maspero and his aides found it was not easy to search tombs when people were living in them. Also, it was difficult to get any information from these tomb dwellers. For centuries they and their ancestors had dug down into the passages, searching the tombs for ancient objects they could sell. Now it was against the law—and this they resented. If they knew anything, they weren't telling. Everyone was innocent.

The break in the case finally came when the police were tipped off that a *fellah* (a poor man) called Abd el-Rasul, from the town of Gurneh, was spending more money than such a person would normally have. Later another man, a fellah also named Abd el-Rasul, was reported to have offered for sale a valuable funerary papyrus.

It was soon apparent that there were several *fellahin* with the surname Abd el-Rasul, all of them brothers, and all of them suspected of dealing in antiquities illegally.

Two were picked up by the police for questioning. These interrogations were not gentle. One of the brothers, Mohammed, had been tied, thrown to the ground, and beaten on the soles of his feet in a futile attempt to make him confess.

Now, alas, history repeated itself: Just as Pawar, the mayor of Western Thebes, came to the aid of the thieves who had ransacked the tombs of the Pharaohs three thousand years before, the mayor and a host of other witnesses swore that the Abd el-Rasul brothers were honest men who had no interest in antiquities and would never, never rob a tomb. The brothers were released.

It seemed sad to Maspero that the prime suspects were deemed innocent and the case closed. Maspero's spirits would have lifted greatly had he known the events that were shortly to erupt.

Mohammed, angry that he had been tortured while his brothers went free and unharmed, demanded from them a higher cut of the loot. He had been getting only one-fifth of the money. Now he demanded half.

At first the others laughed at him. Then the quarrels began. Mohammed became more and more bitter. Angrily he turned informer.

Going secretly to the officials, he told them the truth and offered to lead them to the cache of treasures. Maspero was away, so a German archeologist, Emil Brugsch, and a small retinue of officials accompanied Mohammed to a steep rock cut in the desert.

Tied to the end of a rope, Brugsch was lowered forty feet down a shaft. He found himself in a rough, long corridor. Stumbling along and feeling his way, he came suddenly upon a room that was stacked and packed with royal mummies. His flickering candle shone on the sarcophagi of some of the greatest Pharaohs of ancient Egypt, thirty mummies in all.

Within a few hours rumors ran wild through the nearby town of Gurneh. Royal tombs had been found; there was gold, silver . . .

Men from the town rushed down into the tomb, ready to fight the archeologists and officials for the treasure they thought was there. Guards were brought in. But the archeologists had to move fast if they were to get the royal mummies to the safety of the museum in Cairo.

For eight days and nights they and their crews worked around the clock, moving the sarcophagi and the objects that were left in the tomb. All had to be carried by hand from the mountainside to the Nile River. A heavy sarcophagus required as many as fourteen or fifteen men to carry it, and the trip could take eight hours. It was July and the heat was fierce.

Finally the mummies and whatever funerary treasures were left—papyri, chests, Canopic jars—were loaded on a steamboat, ready for the trip down the Nile to Cairo. As the boat sailed away, people lined the banks of the Nile screaming their grief, placing dust on their heads—just as their ancestors had done thirty centuries before when the kings were taken to their first burial places.

Four Canopic jars bearing the likenesses of the four sons of Horus: the baboon-headed Hapi, the jackal-headed Duamutef, the human headed Imseti, and the falcon-headed Quebusenuef.

Now, headed for their final resting place in the museum, the mummies still were threatened. Partway to Cairo a band of thieves attempted to attack the boat and rob it of its royal cargo. Fortunately they did

A collection of mummies as exhibited at the Egyptian Museum in Cairo at the beginning of the 1900's.

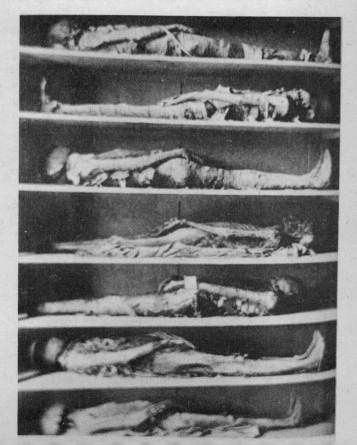

not succeed. The boat was well guarded. But what of the Abd el-Rasul brothers? And how had they discovered the burial chamber in the first place?

The brother Ahmed told the story. Herding his goats, Ahmed found a kid missing. Climbing a steep cut of rock, he discovered an opening into which the kid had fallen. This led to a deep shaft. Later, after he had rescued the kid, he became curious. With a little exploration he soon discovered the great cache of mummies and knew he had found objects of great value.

Ahmed was known to his neighbors as a good and honest man. And he swore when telling the officials his story that he had told only three people about his find: two of his brothers and his son. He also swore that he had gone into the chamber only three times in the ten years he had known of it. And each time he had taken only small objects—figures, little boxes, scarabs, a few papyri—and then only because his family desperately needed money. The officials believed him.

Perhaps the other brothers had been more greedy. However, grateful that the royal mummies had been discovered and safely moved, the government made no charges against the Abd el-Rasuls. In fact, Mohammed, the tortured one who turned informer, was rewarded. He received five hundred pounds in cash and was given a job for life as *rais,* or foreman, of the excavations at Thebes.

7
The Mummy
Unwrappers

The royal mummies were safe in the Cairo Museum. But they were not allowed to rest in peace. The greed of the graverobbers could not disturb them now, but the curiosity of the scientists did. Here was a collection of the great kings of Egypt and their families. What would be found beneath the bandages?

Since the mummies had been robbed in antiquity and the torn bandages repaired by tomb priests, the scholars were not sure how well-preserved the bodies would be. But the ancient priests had done a good job. Three thousand years later the scientists unwrapping the mummies looked upon faces they would have recognized had they known these people in life. And they could tell a few personal things about them, too.

Some of the things were trivial. For example, careful examination of Ramesses II showed that the great king had a skin blemished with blackheads. His successor, Ramesses III, was a very fat man. All mummies look thin, of course, but folds and folds of skin proved the Pharaoh had been obese.

Some of the revelations were more dramatic. King Seqenenre II, the earliest mummy in the group, had met a violent death. There were scalp wounds, one on the side of his head that pierced the skull. Blood still matted his hair, and his face was contorted in an expression of agony. Some believe he was surprised while asleep, and murdered. Others think he was killed in battle, and mummification was done as quickly as possible under difficult circumstances; this would explain the hair still matted with blood. Though killed when in his early thirties, he was already famous as a warrior and known popularly as Seqenenre the Brave.

Of scientific interest to the archeologists was the mummy of a son of Seqenenre. A child when his father was killed, he grew up to become the great Pharaoh Amosis I.

When Amosis I was unwrapped, the scholars were amazed to find that the brain had not been removed in the usual way, through the nostril. Instead, an incision had been made on the left side of the neck, and the atlas vertebra had been removed.

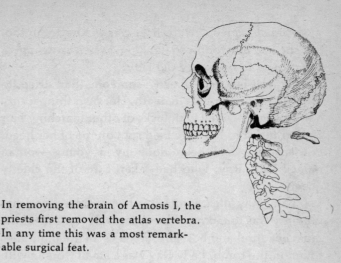

In removing the brain of Amosis I, the priests first removed the atlas vertebra. In any time this was a most remarkable surgical feat.

The brain was then drawn out via the passage that carries the spinal column into the skull (known medically as the *foramen magnum*).

Medical experts questioned that this procedure was possible even with modern surgical knowledge. But it had been done successfully more than thirty centuries ago by some skilled Egyptian, and the mummy of Amosis I was there as proof. However, his is the only mummy ever found in which the brain was removed this way. Why it was done in this difficult fashion, no one knows.

Amosis' queen, Nefertiry, was in the tomb too. But she had long outlived her king. When unwrapped, she proved to be a very old lady.

A well-beloved queen, someone had tried to make her look her best in death. Her own thin, scanty hair was intertwined with locks of other matching hair and arranged to hide the bald spot on top of her head. Perhaps this had been done by a young woman named Lady Ray, who had taken care of the elderly queen.

Lady Ray died soon after her mistress, and her mummy was found near the queen's. It was one of the most beautiful and best-preserved of all the mummies found in the tomb. Lady Ray was a small woman with delicate features, slender hands and feet, and a well-proportioned body. Her heavy hair was dressed in the high fashion of her time: parted in the middle and plaited in narrow braids gathered together in two clusters that framed her face.

After these mummies were brought to Cairo, a smaller cache of royal mummies was also found in the valley and transported to the museum. Among them was Ramesses IV. When his head was unwrapped, those in charge were startled to find that the king had two small onions for eyes.

It was not unusual to find semiprecious stones placed in the eye sockets to heighten the lifelike appearance of the face. But for a Pharaoh who had probably been buried in a solid-gold coffin and adorned with jewels, onions for eyes did seem odd. However, it was said the onions gave a surprisingly realistic effect. And it is known that the onion was highly regarded in ancient Egypt, since it was thought to have magical as well as health-giving powers.

Discovering the royal mummy caches in Egypt gave the scholars in Cairo some famous and interesting mummies to unwrap. But long before these finds, unwrapping mummies had become a popular practice in England.

Mummy unrolling, as it was called, played to packed houses in England as early as 1834. The chief unroller was a prominent London doctor, Thomas J. Pettigrew. Dr. Pettigrew was a professor of anatomy and scientifically interested in the technique of mummification.

He unwrapped his first mummy in the privacy of his own home, slowly, experimentally. But unluckily it was a poor specimen, badly preserved, and he was deeply disappointed.

Fortunately, buying a mummy in England in his day was not too difficult. People of means were interested in collecting Egyptian antiquities and from time to time collections including mummies came onto the market.

Acquiring his second mummy, Pettigrew found that some of his colleagues, as well as archeologists and others, were eager to watch the unrolling. Using the lecture theater at Charing Cross Hospital, where he taught, Dr. Pettigrew for the first time unrolled a mummy for an audience. This mummy was a fine one. And Pettigrew's skill, his comments, and his anatomical explanations held his audience spellbound. Not once in the several hours required for the unrolling was anyone tempted to leave.

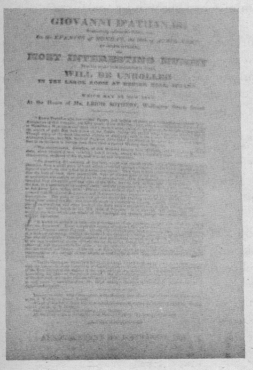

A handbill for a mummy unrolling.

Now it seemed everybody in London, including the great and famous, wanted to see Dr. Pettigrew unwrap a mummy. When it was announced that he would unroll a mummy in the theater of the Royal College of Surgeons on a certain date, it was necessary to issue tickets. Although it was a cold January night, the crowds were so large that even people of great importance couldn't get in. One of the many turned away was the Archbishop of Canterbury!

It became a fashionable pastime to attend Pettigrew unrollings. Tickets were sold, admission charged, handbills printed. Gentlemen and their ladies came dressed as for the theater. Sometimes refreshments were served after the performance. There was a gay party atmosphere.

But in addition, an aura of expectation, almost suspense, filled the hall. There lay the mummy. What would Pettigrew find beneath those bandages tonight?

One amazed audience watched Pettigrew unwrap a mummy that had been gilded over its entire body. While it was not unusual to find mummies with nails, eyelids—even the sexual organs—gilded, the all-golden mummy was unique.

At another of his unrollings Pettigrew removed the outer wrappings and there, placed over the bandaged head and face, was a beautiful portrait of the young man who had died. Painted on a thin board of cedarwood, it was a picture of a youth with large,

The cartonnage of Artemidorous, a Greek living in Roman Egypt, dates back to the second century A. D. Found at Thebes, this cartonnage displays a fine example of a portrait painted on a wood panel. Courtesy of the Trustees of the British Museum.

luminous brown eyes and a delicate oval face. It is one of a group of early portraits from the Graeco/Roman world, and a fine one.

Even the small finds captivated Pettigrew's audiences: the little flower bulbs, their skins still glossy, that were wrapped in the soles of one mummy's feet; the small white onions held in another mummy's hand; on one mummy's breast a sprig of rosemary that looked freshly dried. And of course within the bandages there were amulets, small statues, papyri, sometimes jewelry—which Pettigrew, the showman, displayed for all to see.

One of Pettigrew's mummies turned out to be a fake. The bandages were authentic and he had no reason to believe a proper mummy was not inside them. But when he got inside, he found small piles of sawdust and old rags. There was a long stick for a spine and, oddly enough, vertebrae of a cat. The face was a false face—molded of linen and covered with plaster of Paris.

Some crafty Egyptian, knowing there was a market for mummies, had counterfeited one by filling ancient bandagings with trash.

One mummy gave Pettigrew a bad time. A large audience of about six hundred people filled London's Exeter Hall to see the unrolling. Shortly after Pettigrew started unwrapping, he came upon a layer of very hard substance that enveloped the entire mummy. Pettigrew tried cutting through the dark glassy surface with knives, then with small saws, to no avail. He attacked it with hammers and chisels, but it was harder than rock. Finally the perspiring Pettigrew gave up. He apologized and sent the disappointed audience home.

The doctor became known as Mummy Pettigrew. His public unrollings spread over a period of almost twenty years. The year after his last unwrapping before an audience, Pettigrew had the opportunity to create a mummy.

Alexander, the tenth Duke of Hamilton, who died August 18, 1852, had left instructions that his body was to be mummified. Thirty years before his death, with mummification in mind, the Duke had acquired an ancient sarcophagus in Egypt and shipped it to Hamilton Palace, his estate in England. To hold the sarcophagus, he had a large mausoleum built on the palace grounds. At the Duke's death, Pettigrew was called in to mummify the body. Drawing on the great store of knowledge he had from his years of study and years of unwrapping, Pettigrew followed, as best he knew, the ancient art of mummification.

No one knows, of course, how good a job he did. Duke Alexander rests in peace—a royal English mummy protected from graverobbers and undisturbed by scientific unwrappers.

8
Unwrapping a Mummy in Brooklyn

How does it feel to unwrap a mummy? There is a young man in New York City who knows. He unwrapped one. His name is Kenneth Jay Linsner, and his special interest is the art of ancient Egypt.

At the time he unwrapped the mummy, Ken was working at the Brooklyn Museum as a consultant for conservation in the Department of Egyptian and Classical Art. Ken's job was to restore and protect objects of antiquity. Thus, replacing damaged bandages on a mummy would normally be his aim, rather than removing wrappings.

But Ken felt he could learn a lot by unwrapping a mummy. A young man, just out of his teens, and a keen scholar, he planned how he would go about the task if the museum granted him permission. He would do a thoroughly scientific job, taking his time with the unwrapping, making copious notes. He would measure, study, preserve, and record every step of the way.

Ken knew that this mummy, as far as the museum was concerned, was rather unimportant. What was important to the art museum was the beautiful three-part coffin the mummy lay in, as well as the handsome sarcophagus that held the coffin. These art treasures the museum had bought from the Boston Museum of Fine Arts, back in 1908. The mummy had been acquired incidentally along with the works of art.

While the beautiful coffin and sarcophagus had gotten a great deal of attention in the sixty years they had been in the Brooklyn Museum, the mummy had aroused little interest. Morever, it was not in very good condition. Graverobbers long, long ago had torn some of the wrappings on the body. The Egyptologists at the museum were not sure the body beneath the bandages had been preserved at all. It might be quite worthless. And while it was still in Boston, a mouse had nibbled at the wrappings around its right hip, adding to the damage.

According to the hieroglyphs on the sarcophagus, the mummy was that of a count of Thebes, probably a minor prince. His name was Pa-seba-khai-en-ipet. He lived about 1,000 years before Christ, in the 21st Dynasty.

Ken knew this might or might not be true. Often graverobbers destroyed a body they removed from its sarcophagus or coffin. Then later the empty case, bearing the first mummy's name, was used by another person.

Not long before, Ken had discovered that a handsome cartonnage casing in the museum supposedly containing the mummy of an adult, actually held the body of a child. By means of X-ray detection methods it was found to be the mummy of a little girl eight or nine years old.

So Ken became more and more curious about his mummy. Was it really a Theban count who had lived in the 21st Dynasty? Or a commoner, a man or a woman, who had lived in a later period and had been buried in the count's sarcophagus?

When permission was given Ken to unwrap the mummy, he asked a colleague to help him take it from its coffin to his laboratory. As they carefully lifted it out, Ken remarked, "It's heavier than I thought. Must weigh about fifty pounds."

They carried it into Ken's laboratory and placed it on a long, narrow worktable.

The mummy was still wrapped in an old brown velveteen throw somebody had put around it years before in Boston. Ken removed the throw, folded it, and tossed it on a shelf. It would be handy as a cover

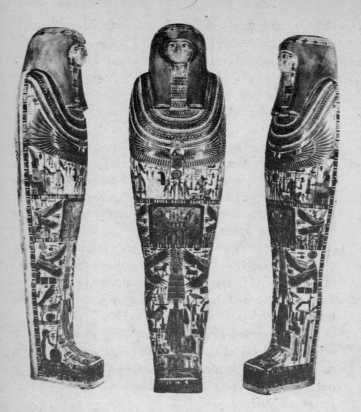

A cartonnage is a case made with layers of linen and gesso using a paper-mache technique formed over a mummiform mold. This cartonnage contains the mummy of Lady Gatsheshen, a child between the ages of eight or nine years. Her body occupies only the lower half of the case; the upper half is packed with loose linen cloth. The Brooklyn Museum, Charles Edwin Wilbour Fund. Brooklyn accession number 34.1223.

for the mummy when he was not working on it.

He looked down at the mummy, somewhat baffled. Where to start?

Ken had tried to find out how other mummy unwrappers had gone about the job in the past. But oddly enough, while a lot had been written on how the ancients *wrapped* a mummy, he could find nothing on how mummies were *unwrapped*. Ken thought surely Dr. Pettigrew, who had done so many unwrappings in England and written a great deal about mummies, would have left some information. But he had written not a word on the subject. And apparently neither had anyone else.

Finally Ken decided to start at the top, on the skull area. The bandages on the head had not been touched. They were in place just as they had been wrapped three thousand years ago. By starting there, he hoped to get the "feel" of unrolling the linen before attacking the areas that had been disturbed and possibly even hastily rewrapped.

The fine condition of the head bandages told Ken that the thieves were probably surprised by guards soon after they had started their looting. For, given time, graverobbers always damaged the head looking for gold earrings and the piece of gold often placed in the mouth.

The tools he chose to use were simple: dental probes, small sharp knives, surgical scissors.

For the first number of days, working very slow-

113

ly, all went well. From the head he stripped off six layers of coarse, loose-weave linen. Beneath these were layers of much finer linen. Then he ran into trouble.

Under the fine linen strips were strips that had been smeared with resin mixed with the chaff of grain and a little sawdust to "bind" it. This had hardened into a substance smooth as glass, hard as rock.

Ken thought of Dr. Pettigrew, who had hit just such a layer of resinous material when he was unwrapping a mummy in London before an audience of hundreds of people, all of whom left, disappointed, when the doctor found he had no instrument with which he could pierce the hard sheath.

The wrapping of a mummy was a ritual. The smallest parts of the body, the hands and feet, were the first to be wrapped; then the head, and finally the trunk of the body.

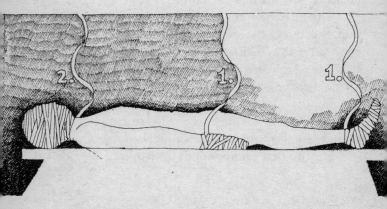

Ken, even as Pettigrew had, tried various small sharp instruments. None of them worked.

A hacksaw would probably do it. But did he dare use such a large, coarse tool on a job so delicate?

He picked up the saw with some misgivings and began working in as small an area as he could, slowly, with great caution. He soon learned to tell by sound and feel where the saw cut through the hard substance and touched the soft bandages. One small area, then another, until bit by bit he had removed the entire resinous layer.

Beneath it he found layers of fragile, pliable linen wrappings. These were exciting to his touch. The other bandages had been dry, somewhat brittle. But these layers, beneath the resin, were still moist with the oils that been applied by priests in sacred rites thirty centuries ago.

Up until now Ken had not thought about the mummy as once having been a living person. The unwrapping had just been an interesting and serious laboratory study. Suddenly it stopped being a laboratory exercise; it became a very human experience.

Beneath the still-moist bandages there was a face. What kind of a face would he find?

Using surgical scissors, he cut a sort of cap of the moist wrappings from the top of the head. He lifted them off. The head was covered with short brownish-red hair.

His mummy was a man. Though the hair receded

115

slightly on the forehead, there was no gray, no baldness. He touched the hair, wondering if it would feel as natural as it looked. It did.

Now he was eager to get on with unwrapping the face. But first, he would make and record measurements of the skull, examining it with care.

On the left side of the head Ken found a small round smooth spot. It was a piece of wax that obviously plugged a hole. With forceps he carefully removed the wax and placed it in a small box. Excited about the find, he called in some of his colleagues. After lengthy discussion they decided the hole could have been made in one of three ways.

First, it might have been made by the embalmers in order to remove the brain. Ken took a probe and gently worked it up into the hole. The hole did not go through into the cranial cavity. No. It had not been a means of removing the brain.

The second theory was that it might have been made accidentally after the man's death. That is, the body might have been dropped or damaged during the process of mummification. This theory could not be tested until the entire body was unwrapped and examined.

The third theory was that it was caused by a blow with a sharp instrument while the man was alive—that it was a death blow. Right from the start Ken was inclined to believe this third theory. But it, too, could

116

not be established until further examination of the body had taken place.

In his eagerness to know more, it was difficult not to hurry with the unwrapping. But much of the scientist's work, if scrupulously done, is painstaking and plodding. And Ken forced himself to continue unwrapping the rest of the head, the face, slowly, methodically, stopping to measure and record.

Eventually he was ready to remove the final facial bandages, which were next to the skin. Then he would know if the mummy had really lived in the 21st Dynasty. For in the 21st Dynasty, and then only for a limited time, the faces of the dead were painted with ochre before the wrapping began: yellow ochre for women, red ochre for men.

With exquisite care he peeled a piece of bandage away from the skin. The skin was red. Now, for the first time, Ken knew that the mummy was a young man who had lived in the 21st Dynasty and that the beautiful coffin and sarcophagus were, undoubtedly, his own.

When he had removed the last of the moist bandages, Ken looked down at the face of his mummy. It was remarkably lifelike. The features were strong and nicely formed. False eyes, painted on linen, the pupils outlined in black, had been placed on his lids. The count had a red-brown beard and moustache. His mouth was firm, the lips well-shaped.

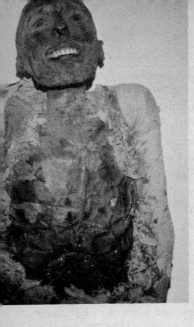

Ken's mummy, Count Pa-seba-khai-en-ipet. The Brooklyn Museum, Brooklyn accession number 08.480.2d.

Would there be a piece of gold in his mouth? Ken doubted it. The lips were slightly parted, and he could see no gold. There was a packing of some kind, though.

Picking up an instrument, he carefully probed the mouth. It was lightly packed with linen, which he removed. The linen was still moist with oil, probably butter, which the Egyptians often used for this purpose. He placed the material in a box, taking time to label it and make a record.

He was interested in examining the teeth. For one thing, they often told a lot about a person's age.

The teeth were remarkable—straight and sound, all in fine condition. Even the lowers were only slightly worn. Ken decided the Theban count had died when he was in his early or middle thirties.

The only jewelry he wore were gold earrings. Slipping them from the mummy's ears, Ken saw they were of fairly simple but pleasing design, typical of the work done by 21st-Dynasty goldsmiths. The Count of Thebes had not ranked high in royalty, though he probably had been a minor prince.

A small plug filled each ear. These, too, Ken removed, placed in a box, and recorded.

A wax ear plug taken from the ear of Ken's mummy. It still bears the impression of the outer ear. The Brooklyn Museum, Brooklyn accession number 08.480.2e.

The nostrils were also filled with plugs. When Ken removed them, he saw that peppercorns were mixed in the waxy substance. He held several of them in his hand, looking at the small round berries that had been plucked from a growing pepper plant three thousand years ago to be used in a mummification rite.

Curious, Ken placed them on a slide. With a scalpel he sectioned them, and dropped water on one half with a pipette. To his amazement they "revived" after thirty centuries and gave off the same spicy fragrance of our fresh peppercorns today.

The mummy's nose was so straight, so nicely shaped, that Ken wondered if the brain had been extracted in the usual way: by breaking through the ethmoid bone and drawing it out via the nostril. Using a long, slender instrument, he probed up into the cranial cavity. He found it had. Ken's mummy was one more example of the ancient Egyptian's skill in performing this delicate operation of brain removal.

No wonder these people excelled in the field of medicine—so much so that men from other countries came to Egypt to learn, and when a great man far away fell ill, they often sent to Egypt for a doctor! In an age when cutting the human body—either dead or alive—was forbidden in other lands, the Egyptians, through their practice of mummification, learned an enormous amount about the physical make-up of man. The operator who cut the embalming wound, then severed and removed the major organs, must have been well learned in anatomy, as was the skilled man who removed the brain. In addition, the very process of mummification gave the Egyptians an opportunity to examine the bodies of people just dead and a chance to study the causes of death, diseases, and abnormalities.

Ken could imagine that the hole in his mummy's head had undoubtedly been studied by those who were wrapping the corpse, and a diagnosis made.

As he worked along, peeling away the bandages, taking care not to shatter the brittle ones or tear the moister fragile ones, he began to find thousands of tiny dead bugs and beetles in the wrappings. Insects had laid their eggs on the linens while the body was being wrapped. The little bugs had hatched later and died, imprisoned in the strips of cloth.

He found no amulets.

As the days and weeks went by and the work progressed, Ken became more and more pleased with the condition of his mummy. Removing the bandages, little by little, he wondered if he would come upon parts that were poorly preserved. He never did. When he unwrapped the chest area, where the tomb robbers had torn the bandages, he found this too intact. The thieves had damaged only the outer cloth. They must have been scared off early in the game.

Actually, the Boston mouse, nibbling through the wrappings on the hip, had done more damage than the thieves.

People began to hear about the young man who was unwrapping a mummy. They wanted to watch. At the start he tried to be generous with his time and his mummy, and he let a few people into his small laboratory.

"What is his name?" they often asked.

"Pa-seba-khai-en-ipet," Ken answered.

"But what do you *call* him? Haven't you given him a nickname?"

"No," said Ken. "He has no nickname. His name is Pa-seba-khai-en-ipet."

A nickname had never entered Ken's mind. It seemed to him that this man who had lived three thousand years ago and died a violent death deserved the dignity of being called by his full and proper name.

One woman came with a moneymaking proposition. If Ken would move his mummy from the small laboratory into the museum auditorium, she would round up an audience of friends and members of her garden club. They would pay to watch an unwrapping session, and the money would be given as a donation to the museum. Although Ken knew that the great mummy scholar Pettigrew had unrolled mummies to paying audiences more than a hundred years earlier in London, he turned the lady down.

But when people were seriously interested and he could accommodate them, Ken often did.

However, he avoided interruptions whenever possible, for unwrapping the mummy was necessarily a sparetime job with Ken. As a student at New York University he was carrying a full schedule, working toward a degree. In addition he had his regular job at the museum in the Department of Ancient Arts.

Thus he worked on the mummy when he could—usually late afternoons and on Saturdays and Sundays. He really had no time for interruptions from curiosity-seekers.

Sometimes, interruptions could not be avoided. Once there was a period of several days when work went slowly because of frequent knockings on the laboratory door. A banquet was to be held at the museum one night for Israel's premier, Golda Meir, who was visiting the United States. Great security measures were taken for her protection everywhere she went.

Now, a museum has a lot of hiding places and many rooms that are dark at night. So for days before the banquet the security chief of the museum received security guards and policemen from the F.B.I., the Secret Service, and the New York City police, who were checking "behind-the-scenes" spots in the huge building.

Ken's laboratory was one of these spots. Each time a guard or a policeman came in and found a young man unwrapping a mummy, he was, of course, intrigued. Each time, Ken politely showed him the mummy. Each time, the visiting officer was interested most in the hole in the mummy's head. And every man made the same comment: "Just exactly the size a .38 caliber bullet would make!"

Ken decided that if there had been guns and .38 caliber bullets in the year 1000 B.C., that might have been just what killed the count. He became more and more sure, as the unwrapping neared completion, that death had been caused by a murderous blow with a sharp instrument. An accident after death, during mummification, he ruled out because there were no signs of damage or carelessness on the body. Also, this man had lived in a time of great political turmoil and skulduggery in Egypt. Even a minor prince might well have had enemies who would profit by his death.

There came the day when Ken removed the last piece of bandage. He looked at his mummy with pride and satisfaction. It was in excellent condition. The limbs were straight, the hands and feet—and their nails—intact. Even the genital organs were in a perfect state of preservation.

Here was a man about five and a half feet tall, broad of shoulder for his height, strong and well formed. A personable, good-looking man who undoubtedly had had friends. But who also had had enemies and been murdered by them. Ken could feel sad that this young man of Thebes, with his reddish-

124

brown hair and matching beard and moustache, had died before his time, violently.

Obviously he couldn't keep Pa-seba-khai-en-ipet indefinitely in the small laboratory. For one thing, in order to preserve the unwrapped body, it must be kept in an atmosphere of even temperature and humidity.

"Why can't he be put on display in the museum in a case?" one young man asked.

The reason: The Brooklyn Museum is a museum of art. The mummy may be an object of great interest, but he is not an object of art. The elegant tripartite coffin, of course, *is*—and it is on display.

The practical solution was to put the count in a carefully guarded and controlled storage area in the museum. This area is not open to the public. It is kept locked and strictly guarded. Even those working in the museum find it is not simple to gain entrance.

Now that Ken has left the Brooklyn Museum, it is doubtful that the mummy receives much attention. But there, today, lies Pa-seba-khai-en-ipet, on a shelf of his own, wrapped in his old brown velveteen throw.

9
Where Did All
the Mummies Go?

A mummy must be pretty tough.

We have seen how the thirty royal mummies survived the damage by graverobbers, the hasty rewrapping by tomb priests, a hurried transfer to another tomb in antiquity, and finally, in modern times, the trip by boat to Cairo. Even unwrapped, a mummy will continue to exist if kept with reasonable care, the temperature constant, humidity low.

Why then, out of the tremendous number of mummies made by the ancient Egyptians over a period of twenty-five centuries, are there only a comparatively few left? Obviously, they were destroyed.

Some were destroyed by carelessness and ignorance, some by accident. A few, a very few, were destroyed in scientific study and experimentation. But many were destroyed on purpose, for profit.

The greatest destruction of mummies for profit occurred over a period of four hundred years, when mummies were used as medicine. From the early thirteenth century A.D. well into the seventeenth century, Egyptian tombs were stripped of their mummies, the mummies chopped up and sold in Europe to be fed to the sick and ailing.

While the ancient thieves favored the tombs of the royal and the rich, these later looters took any and all mummies they could find. For them, the communal tombs of the poor, stacked with mummies, were bonanzas.

Taking "mummy" to cure their ills was not just a practice of the superstitious and ignorant. Far from it! Sir Francis Bacon, the great English philosopher of Shakespeare's day, took it and recommended it particularly "for the staunching of blood." Whether Shakespeare used it or not, we don't know. But he mentions it as medicine in several of his plays. And it is one of the magic ingredients in the witches' brew in *Macbeth*.

King François I of France always carried a little packet of mummy in case of sudden illness or an accident.

Most all the doctors of those centuries prescribed it and believed in it as a cure for many diseases.

The loathsome practice would never have gotten started if people had known how mummies were really made. They thought bitumen—a kind of mineral pitch—was used in the wrappings to preserve the bodies. It never was. What they saw in the wrappings was not bitumen but resins that had turned black and glasslike, resembling the mineral.

For several centuries before they began using cut-up mummies for medicine, pure bitumen was prized as a cure-all. However, it was hard to get. There was a mountain in Persia where bitumen, called

This child, who probably lived during the 2nd Dynasty, was not mummified and yet was largely preserved through the drying nature of the sand and the sun's heat.

mummia by the Persians, oozed out of cracks in the rocks. It was considered so precious, the mountain was guarded night and day and the mineral was stored in the Royal Treasury. There were other sources—the Dead Sea, for one. But these sources were very difficult to work, and the amounts extracted after tremendous hard labor were small.

Doctors, apothecaries, the sick, and the suffering demanded it. Merchants dishonestly stretched the precious stuff by mixing it with pitch. Smugglers and thieves trafficked in it. Another source was desperately needed.

Then came the rumor, wild and inaccurate: In Egypt there were thousands, probably hundreds of thousands, of ancient bodies wrapped in bandages that were heavy with bitumen. Travelers had seen them. Why not remove the bandages and reclaim the substance?

At the very first this is what was done. The body itself was not used. And because the Persians called the substance mummia, the Arabs began calling the bandaged body a mummy. Thus the word mummy was never known to the Egyptians who practiced mummification. It was coined in the early centuries after Christ. It is actually a misnomer for a wrapped corpse.

As soon as the "bitumen" (which was really resin) from the wrappings came into use, doctors and surgeons everywhere proclaimed it far better, far more effective, than the natural bitumen, or mummia, had ever been. It was believed that the human body around which it had been wrapped gave the drug, in some unknown way, greater curing powers. Now the doctors asked: If this is so, why not go one step further and use the entire wrapped body?

Without doubt, those who dealt in the drug found it much easier to chop up the whole mummy. It must have been a bit difficult to unwrap the body, soak the bandages, and reclaim the hard black substance. Also, there would be a much greater volume of salable drug if the whole body were used.

A lot was needed! Not only did doctors prescribe mummy for all kinds of ailments and diseases, but also for bone fractures, concussions, paralysis—even as an antidote for poison. It became a standard drug on the shelves of apothecary shops all over Europe.

Demand was so great, so many mummies were being destroyed to make the drug, that Egyptian officials finally realized along in the late sixteenth century that their land would soon be mummyless if steps weren't taken. So it was made illegal to transport mummies. They must be left in their tombs.

This led to a most unsavory fraud, practiced on a wide and dangerous scale in Egypt. Greedy and dishonest men began to manufacture mummies. They took any bodies they could lay their hands on. Some were executed criminals. Others were slaves who had died and whose bodies had not been claimed. Some were paupers who had died without funds or friends to bury them.

These facts mattered not at all to the mummy manufacturers as they went about the business of making a mummy. First they filled the body's natural openings with a cheap blackish material, asphaltum. Then incisions were cut in the muscular part of the limbs and asphaltum packed in. The bodies were then tightly bound up and placed in the sun. The heat of the sun and the arid atmosphere dried them out sufficiently so they looked like mummies. And as mummies they were sold.

A prominent French physician, visiting Egypt late in the sixteenth century, saw one of these "mummy factories." He reported that he saw forty or more mummies newly made and ready for sale. He asked the owner of the factory if any of these people had died of infectious diseases, especially the plague. The owner said he neither knew nor cared. As long as he could get the bodies, it mattered not to him how the person died. These were the bodies that would turn up as mummies in apothecary jars in Europe!

When the physician returned to France, he told a friend, a well-known surgeon, what he had seen. They both publicly denounced the use of mummy as medicine and refused to prescribe it. Whether they influenced others in their profession is not known.

In any event, the use of mummy as medicine was

on its way out. But not because the medical men and their patients had lost faith in it as a cure-all.

The fraudulent mummy-makers in Egypt were in trouble. It started in one small town where money was sorely needed to meet local expenses. The town officials learned that a certain citizen was getting rich making false mummies and transporting them for sale. They had him arrested, fined him a large sum, and let him go. But not for long. A few mummies later he was again arrested and again the fine was a big one.

Other towns and cities heard of this simple method of raising funds and tried it—with success. Soon the heavy fines became too much for the crooks. They could not afford to continue their mummy hoax and went out of business. With no mummies available—real or false—mummy as medicine gradually disappeared.

But for a long time after, the mummia from Mummy Mountain in Persia was still considered magical and more precious than gold. In 1809 the King of Persia, wishing to bestow an important gift on the Queen of England and the Empress of Russia, sent each lady a small gold box full of the bitumen. While traveling in Persia a few years later, Sir William Ouseley, an English writer, met a trader who offered a dab of the mountain's mummia—about enough to fill an English walnut shell—for the price of eight pounds sterling. He did not buy it. The price was too high.

The hand of a Ptolemaic mummy.

How many mummies were destroyed to make the drug called mummy is not known. But during the four centuries or more that the medical craze existed, the number used for this purpose must have been staggering.

However, the mummy medicine makers and the graverobbers were not the only guilty ones. Large numbers of mummies, especially those buried in communal tombs, were destroyed by curiosity-seekers, by careless tourists whose hobby was Egyptian antiquities, and even by men who considered themselves serious Egyptologists.

Among the guiltiest of these latter was an Italian named Giovanni Belzoni. Originally a professional strongman, he went to England to perform in shows. There he became interested in Egyptian archeology.

He was a huge man—more than six and a half feet tall, broad and brawny. And in Egypt, early in the nineteenth century, his mode of exploring for antiquities was apparently as brash as he was big.

Belzoni wrote of his experience, discovering long passageways that tunneled into mountainsides where large numbers of mummies had been buried, stacked in their wooden cases. In his own words:

A vast quantity of dust rises, so fine that it enters into the throat and nostrils, and chokes the nose and mouth to such a degree that it requires great power of lungs to resist it and the strong effluvia of the mummies. . . . In such a situation I found myself several times, and often returned exhausted and fainting . . . . Though fortunately I am destitute of the sense of smelling, I could taste that the mummies were rather unpleasant to swallow. After the exertion of entering into such a place, through a passage of fifty, a hundred, three hundred, or perhaps six hundred yards, nearly overcome I sought a resting place, found one and contrived to sit. But when my weight bore on the body of an Egyptian, it crushed it like a band-box. I naturally had recourse to my hands to sustain my weight, but they found no better support. So that I sunk altogether among the broken mummies, with a crash of bones, rags and wooden cases, which raised such a dust as kept me motionless for a quarter of an hour, waiting till it subsided. I could not remove from the place, however, without increasing it and every step I took I crushed a mummy. . . .

Another time Belzoni describes finding a passageway so filled with mummies, there was scarcely room for him to force his way through.

"It was choked with mummies," he wrote. "I could not pass without putting my face in contact with some decayed Egyptians. But my own weight helped me on. However, I could not avoid being covered with bones, legs and arms and heads rolling from above."

The toll of mummies taken by Belzoni's shocking unconcern alone must have been very large.

On a much smaller scale, there was a time when mummies were destroyed by being ground into powder for use by European artists. During the Renaissance artists believed that if they added mummy powder to their pigments, the paint would not crack on the canvas.

It is known, too, that at times poor people in

Egypt unwrapped the mummies, discarded the body, and used the resin-soaked bandages for fuel. There is a record, made in 1817, stating that the people in the treeless land of Thebes, lacking kindling, burned mummy wrappings in their small ovens.

No one knows how many mummies were victims of paper manufacturers! Paper made from cloth, so-called rag paper, has always been of high quality and in demand. And if the mummy cloth was not heavily impregnated with resins, the wrappings would be very useful for this purpose. It was not unusual for 150 yards of cloth to be used in wrapping a single mummy—and sometimes a great deal more. When the Pharaoh Ramesses III was unwrapped, it was estimated that about 350 yards of cloth had been used.

There is evidence that a nomadic tribe in Egypt, the Bedouins, stole mummies and sold the bandages for papermaking. And there are documents to prove that an American paper manufacturer, one Augustus Stanwood, who owned a paper mill in Maine, imported mummies during the latter part of the nineteenth century for this purpose.

Unfortunately, many of the wrappings on the mummies shipped to Maine were darkly stained with resin. Mr. Stanwood tried to bleach them so he could make high-grade paper. But he failed. Not wanting to waste the mummy cloth, he used it for making ordinary brown wrapping paper, which he sold in rolls to butchers and grocers. In those days food did

not come packaged. Hence housewives were unknowingly getting their meat, butter, bread, and groceries
wrapped in paper made from mummy bandages.

Then there was an outbreak of cholera. The
epidemic was traced to the rag cutters and pickers in
Stanwood's paper mill. The mummy wrappings were
blamed, and Mr. Stanwood's papermaking scheme
ended.

Thus from the ancient days of the tomb robbers
on, mummies were wantonly destroyed.

Even in relatively recent times the destruction has
continued. A rare mummy, one of the oldest ever
found, was thought to be safe in the Museum of the
Royal College of Surgeons in England. Dating back to
2300 B.C., the mummy had survived graverobbers, the
medicine makers, and other threats for more than
forty centuries. But he was destroyed during the blitz
on London in World War II when a German bomb hit
the museum in 1941 and blew him to bits.

Some mummies in modern times have been
unavoidably destroyed for scientific study. But mummies lost in this way are few.

An English scientist, Sir Marc Armand Ruffer,
decided back in 1909 that it would be possible to learn
about diseases in ancient Egypt by studying mummy
pieces under a microscope. Actually, when he began
his work, Ruffer did not need whole, intact mummies.
If they were in good condition, he could use parts of
mummies that had been shattered or broken.

Ruffer coined a long and impressive—but logical—word for his studies: paleopathology (combining the Greek word *paleo,* meaning ancient, with *pathology,* the study of disease).

Right at the start Ruffer ran into trouble. When he tired to cut off fragments of mummy tissue to place under his microscope, he found the tissue so hard that the blades of his sharp microtome knives broke. He had to find a way of restoring some flexibility to the pieces without damaging the tissue.

Ruffer finally devised a process of soaking and chemical treatment that restored the flinty mummy fragments into manageable pieces. He had no trouble now cutting them into sections—as he could have done with fresh tissue—and placing them in paraffin for study under the microscope.

He was amazed! Body tissues twenty-five or more centuries old "came alive" enough for Ruffer to study the mummies' blood vessels and arteries, their skin, mammary glands, testicles, viscera. Fortunately, Ruffer had access to some mummies most of which were of the 21st Dynasty (about 1080—946 B.C.), when Canopic jars were temporarily not used and the organs were embalmed, wrapped in linen, and returned to the body. Thus he had a chance to examine microscopically sections of liver, stomach, kidneys, lungs.

How had these people died? Ruffer found that the ancient Egyptians suffered from some of the same diseases we have today. In the skin of one middle-aged man of the 18th Dynasty Ruffer found pustular-like eruptions, which he diagnosed as smallpox virus. In sections of a kidney he recognized bacilli which told him the person had suffered from kidney abscesses.

One of the mummies had worked or lived in an atmosphere where the air was heavily polluted, probably by smoke. His lung tissue, under the microscope, was pitted, imbedded with soot, and inflamed—signs of anthracosis, a disease that is prevalent today among coal miners.

Tiny egg-shaped bacilli, characteristic of the plague, were found in the tissue of a liver.

Ruffer succeeded so well in "restoring" pieces of mummy, he decided to experiment with solutions in which he could soak the whole mummy. He succeeded in this too. He reported that the mummy was so easily handled, he was able to run his fingers along the intermuscular walls separating the muscles from one another to expose the nerves, ligaments, joints, and cartilages so they were easily seen. With these mummies he was also able to remove the large arteries for study.

Apparently the arteries held special fascination for Ruffer. He found many cases of calcification, indicating that these people had suffered from severe hardening of the arteries—one of the leading causes of strokes and death today.

As Ruffer's experiments exposed the very skeleton of the mummy, he was also able to study the bones of these people, and found that a great many early Egyptians suffered from arthritis. There was a very high rate of bone and joint deterioration. Broken bones were not uncommon. And though the ancient Egyptian doctor was usually very skillful at setting and treating fractures, Ruffer did report one broken leg, a thigh (femur) bone, that had "been deplorably set." However, he later ascertained that the victim was a soldier, and probably the job had been hastily done under difficult combat conditions.

All in all, Ruffer destroyed very few mummies in his experiments, and surely his interesting scientific findings justified the loss.

Today, in Egypt, mummies are protected as objects of antiquity. It is illegal to send one out of Egypt without an authorization from the Department of Antiquities. A museum in another country might find it possible to buy a mummy and get permission from the department to ship it out for its collection, but this would be very difficult for an individual to do.

Even if a tourist from the United States were able to buy a mummy in Egypt and managed somehow to have it shipped home, he would find it virtually impossible to get it into the United States. For the U.S. Customs Bureau considers a mummy a dead body—which indeed it is. Moreover, it is a dead body without any of the necessary papers for entrance into

This man died of a sword cut to the skull. His remains were found in the Byzantine Cemetery at Hesa in Nubia.

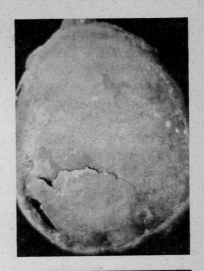

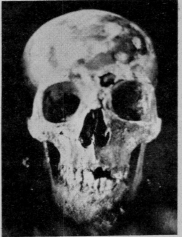

Another skull also shows a sword wound made just before death. It, too, was found in the Byzantine Cemetery at Hesa.

the U.S.A. It has no passport, no doctor's statement as to cause of death, no death certificate.

If it were classified as a work of art, entrance would be simple. But a mummy is not a work of art. Technically it is an anthropological specimen. And as such, it can legally enter the country only if its destination is the anthropological department of a recognized museum or university.

These regulations are very hard for the tourist who would like to add a mummy to his collection. But they help enormously to keep the mummies where they belong: in Egypt.

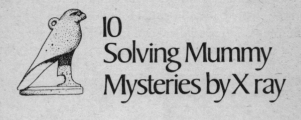

10
Solving Mummy
Mysteries by X ray

In 1895 a German physicist named Roentgen discovered a new kind of ray which he named the X ray, and a machine was developed that for the first time permitted man to "see" through opaque objects.

Shortly after the X-ray machine came into use, some Egyptologists realized that here was a means of examining mummies without unwrapping them. However, for a long time it was not practical. An X-ray machine was a large, complicated permanent installation—and very expensive. It was, of course, of paramount importance for hospitals and clinics to install these machines; for medical men they opened a whole new world in diagnosis and treatment of human ills. But a museum—where the mummies were—could scarcely afford to put in one of the great contraptions to look at bodies of people who had been dead for two thousand years and more.

Occasionally a museum curious about a particular mummy would ask a hospital for permission to use its equipment and would take the mummy there for X

This man's decapitated head was ingeniously secured to the body by means of a stick thrust into the skull and neck, and then bandages were specially wrapped to prevent the head from nodding or twisting.

rays. This, of course, could be done only on a very limited scale. Then, in recent years, a kind of streamlined X-ray machine was developed. It was portable, so it could be taken to the mummies. And it was powerful enough to "look" down through the bandages and record a picture of what it saw.

One of the first men to X-ray mummies and report what he found was an English scholar, P. H. K. Gray, who acquired a portable machine in 1964 and asked permission to photograph the mummies in the British Museum in London. There were seventy-eight mummies there, twenty-four of them children and infants.

Gray was very pleased with the pictures his machine took. He said the bones, inside the bandages, looked much the same as X-ray pictures of living people would. And the X rays told him a lot about the aches and pains suffered by ancient Egyptians. He found (as Ruffer had found from his microscopic examinations of mummies) that the Egyptians were plagued with many of the same ailments we have today.

Some of these miseries, he learned, had hit the Egyptians at a younger age. He figured that most of the adults were on the youngish side—not over forty years of age. Yet fifteen of them had been afflicted with osteoarthritis, a condition we sometimes call rheumatism, and which we associate with the aging process and today find mostly in the elderly.

His pictures revealed diseased disks of the spine, indicating severe backaches. Several of the mummies had gallstones. He learned that some of the people had experienced either malnutrition or a serious illness while they were growing up, as the photographs detected evidence of arrested growth. And the pictures of one baby showed that the infant had suffered from a rare disorder in which the bones did not develop normally, diagnosed today as *osteogenesis imperfecta.*

The Egyptians had known, all too well, the agony of toothaches. X rays detected many caries, or cavities, missing teeth, and diseases of the gums.

But the pictures revealed more than physical conditions and ailments. Photographs of one mummy made a surprising discovery that still cannot be explained. The wrapped figure was of large size. And with reason! It proved to be not one but four mummies! There was the body of a big-boned man. Bandaged with him were two infants, probably twins, each placed on one of the man's thighs. Then a child, a boy about ten years old, lay head downward on its side along the man's right leg.

It was not uncommon to find the mummy of a newborn infant buried with its mother. Presumably the mother had died after giving birth to a stillborn child. But why would two babies and a small boy be placed within the wrappings of a man? No one could hazard a guess.

Hawk amulet; the Isis knot; Ram
amulet; Screech Baboon holding
"the Eye of Horus"; a late amulet
combining four "Eye of Horus",
papyrus stalks and a rosette; and
the Djed Pillar symbol of the
backbone of Osiris.

Of interest, too, were the amulets and jewelry, even rolls of papyrus, wrapped within the bandages that showed up on the pictures. At first the exact location, or depth within the bandages, of these objects was not clear. Gray found that by using a fluorescent screen of an X-ray intensifier, it was possible to locate the amulets precisely.

When the mummies in the British Museum were all photographed, Gray moved his portable unit to Liverpool, where there were sixteen Egyptian mummies in the city museum. One of the Liverpool mummies Gray decided to "rob."

From the photographs he could tell that the mummy was in such poor condition, it was scarcely worth preserving. And on the pictures, Gray counted thirty-two amulets, plus a long string of beads and some rolls of papyrus that could be salvaged.

What the X-ray pictures did not tell him and his helpers was that the resin in which these objects had been placed had become so hard, it was to be an almost impossible task to remove the imbedded amulets. Each amulet had to be tediously chipped from its hard setting, with care taken not to damage it or others wrapped near it. And thirty of the amulets were wrapped in the bandages covering the chest area.

Each one, finally, was removed safely after many hours of patient and skillful work. Some were beautifully made, others rather roughly fashioned. All but one were carved of hard stone. This collection of amulets, plus the beads and papyrus, was considered of sufficient interest to justify unwrapping one mummy in very poor condition. And even the mummy was not lost—it was used in mummy research.

While the Englishman Gray was X-raying mummies in the London and Liverpool museums, two young Americans were in Egypt with portable X-ray equipment. They were about to embark on one of the most exciting mummy studies ever undertaken: photographing a group of royal mummies, which had not been unwrapped, in the museum in Cairo.

The two young men were James E. Harris, a scientist and orthodontist interested in genetics, and Kent R. Weeks, an archeologist. Actually, their work in Egypt started far from Cairo and was not even remotely connected with photographing royal mummies.

A group of dentists at the University of Michigan's School of Dentistry wanted to do a study on the development of teeth in mankind over the past thousand or more years. A remote spot in Nubia, hundreds of miles south of Cairo, was selected for the study. It was chosen because a research expedition was there excavating the site of seven cemeteries that had existed over a period of almost two thousand years. There were more than five thousand skeletons—not mummies—excavated and available for study. These remains dated from about the first century A.D. to the eighteenth century A.D.

For the two young Americans the Nubian project was hard, grubby work: examining skeletons, studying the teeth, measuring jaws and bone structure, taking bone and tissue samples for laboratory study, keeping voluminous notes and records.

When they finished in Nubia, they decided to go to Thebes with new portable X-ray units that had just been developed at the University of Michigan and photograph—for comparison with the Nubians—the teeth of mummies there. Excited by the X-ray pictures of the mummies in Thebes, they asked the museum in Cairo for permission to photograph the royal mummies, and permission was granted.

Harris and Weeks have written and illustrated, with photographs, a book on their work, called *X-raying the Pharaohs*, published by Charles Scribner's Sons, 1972. It tells in fascinating detail their experiences, how they photographed the mummies and what they found.

They discovered, as Gray did with the mummies in England, that the ancient Egyptians usually did not live to be very old; that they suffered from toothaches, arthritis, backaches, much as people do today.

But there were other major findings revealed by the powerful portable unit. The young ruler, Siptah, who died when he was about twenty, had been described throughout history as having had a club-foot. The X rays indicated, rather, that Siptah had had polio, probably when he was a child, leaving the foot deformed. And the X rays showed clearly that the right leg was foreshortened, the soft tissue wasted away—signs of poliomyelitis or as laymen often call it, infantile paralysis.

From a medical standpoint this was an important discovery. While up until now this is the only suspected case of polio detected in an Egyptian mummy, if the diagnosis is correct, it tells us that this crippling disease existed as long ago as 1200 B.C.

The most startling discovery Harris and Weeks made with their X-ray unit—and certainly the one that got the most popular response—was their photograph of the small mummy buried with the powerful queen, or high priestess, Makare.

Makare's mummy had been unwrapped and examined long before, and a description of it was included in a book published in 1924, *Egyptian Mummies*, by the Egyptologists G. E. Smith and Warren R. Dawson. They knew that Makare had died either in childbirth or shortly after a baby was born. And buried with her in her tomb was the small mummy assumed to be her child.

The baby mummy was not unwrapped. Was it a boy? A girl? How old was the infant? These questions were frequently asked, and Smith and Dawson, in their book, long ago voiced the hope that someday a radiograph could be made of the small mummy and its identity cleared.

More than forty years later, in 1966, this was done when Harris and Weeks photographed the mummy with their X-ray machine. They found it was neither a boy nor a girl child. It was a female baboon. Now everyone asked: "Why would an animal mummy be placed in the tomb of Makare? And why a baboon?"

It is true that the baboon in ancient Egypt had some sacred significance and was associated with Thoth, the god of learning. But the Egyptians also

Thoth, the god of learning, and the sacred baboon.

related many other animals to their gods and religion. Those animals, birds, even reptiles and fish, that were identified with certain gods were commonly mummified in Egypt. Their mummies were sold and entombed as votive offerings to the gods.

An ibis mummy in elaborate wrappings found in the ibis cemetery at Abydos.

A Graeco/Roman mummy of a cat.

Each creature had its own separate cemetery, one of the most famous of which is the Cemetery of the Sacred Bulls in Saqqara. Today one can walk along the great underground passageway, between the rows of colossal sarcophagi, each of which once held the mummy of a sacred bull. Alas, all are empty. The bulls, having great religious importance, were buried with riches, and every sarcophagus was robbed. Lesser beasts and birds, buried without treasure, survived in their beautifully wrought and decorated coffins, which are prized today as minor works of art.

A mummified bull.

But these mummified animals—large and small—were always buried with their own kind. Nor was it a practice to put the mummy of a beast in the tomb of a human. So again, the question: Why was the mummy of a baboon placed in the tomb of the great high priestess?

There is no certain answer.

One theory is that Makare died but her baby lived. The baboon was mummified and buried with her to replace, symbolically, her own child. This is an appealing explanation and it may or may not be true. But in any event, Mr. Harris and Mr. Weeks, with their portable X-ray machine, cleared up the identity of the tiny mummy in Makare's tomb.

The use of X rays in studying mummies, as time goes on, may help answer many questions and solve other mysteries. Certainly it will literally bring to light a whole fresh store of knowledge about the ancient Egyptians, how they lived and how they died.

II
"Mummies" of Caves, Bogs, and Mountains

mummy /'məm-ē/ *n* [ME *mummie* powdered parts of mummified body used as a drug. fr. MF *momie,* fr. ML *mumia* mummy, powdered mummy, fr. Ar *mūmiyah* bitumen, mummy, fr. Per *mūm* wax] <u>1 a : a body embalmed or treated for burial with preservatives after the manner of the ancient Egyptians</u> b : a body unusually well preserved 2 : one resembling a mummy — mummy *vb*

This first definition is what we have meant in this book by a mummy.

But all over the world there have been other preserved bodies popularly called mummies. Some of these have been preserved completely by nature. In others nature had some assistance from man. But none of these so-called mummies was bandaged or wrapped as a true Egyptian mummy was.

The Egyptians themselves had bodies preserved in the hot, dry sand long before they began mummification. And after the need for mummification ceased—when Christianity was introduced into Egypt—there were bodies preserved by nature, called Coptic mummies.

The name Coptic refers to a branch of Christianity that has existed in Egypt since the first few centuries after the birth of Christ.

The Coptic mummies were not so remarkable for their own state of preservation as for the clothes they wore. True, the bodies lying in their hot, dry graves were fairly well-preserved. But the clothes they were dressed in were of greater interest than the bodies themselves. Intricately woven and beautifully embroidered, the garments—buried for fifteen hundred years and more—were in such a fine state of preservation that after being carefully washed in soap and water, they were as bright and lovely as new. Moreover, the fine leather boots, decorated in glowing colors, were cleaned and restored to their original beauty. Examples of these clothes and the colorful boots can now be seen in the Cairo Museum.

As well-dressed as the Coptic mummies were, nowhere in the world were there mummies as magnificently gowned as the royal mummies of Peru.

These were the bodies of Inca rulers. The mummies, deified and worshipped by the Indians, were of great religious significance to the people. And they were kept, resplendent on their golden thrones, in the Temple of the Sun, high in the mountains at Cuzco.

Cuzco is more than 11,000 feet above sea level, and while the yearly rainfall of the Andean Highlands would prevent natural mummification, the dry air in the various rock tombs did help in the preservation of a body. And on the arid coast of Peru there have survived complete and elaborate mummy bundles from pre-Inca cultures dating back at least as far as 1400 B.C.

In any event, after the viscera was removed from the deceased ruler and herbs used in the drying-out process, the mummified body was clothed in splendid royal raiment and seated on a golden throne in the palace. After a period of mourning in which a few favorite servants let themselves be voluntarily strangled to be with their king, the throne and the king were carried into the Temple of the Sun where he was placed alongside other regally-robed kings and queens who had died before him.

With their arms crossed in front of them, their eyes cast down, they sat on their thrones looking much as they had in life. Revered as rulers, they were worshipped by the people as gods. On state occasions and for great religious festivals, they were carried, on their thrones, out into the streets and squares, and paraded before the crowds. The people fell to their knees before them, weeping and crying out words of reverence and adoration.

All this ended when the Spanish explorer, Pizarro, and his army invaded Peru early in the sixteenth century in their ruthless search for gold and treasures. It was expected that the Spaniards would rob the royal mummies. But robbing them was not enough.

The burial raiment of an ordinary citizen of the Cuzco region was often a simple skin sack into which the body was sewn.

Pre-Inca mummy bundles frequently had false heads remarkably decorated with eyes and noses and mouths. These false heads made of cloth bundles also present an unsolved puzzle for scientists. Perhaps they have something to do with the fact that many mummies had no heads, having lost them in battle. Then, too, there was an extraordinary trophy head cult in which the head of an enemy might symbolically be placed on the mummy bundle of a dead warrior. Then, again, the false heads might serve to keep the deceased in touch with the world of the living. They remain a mystery.

Scientists to this day do not know the significance of the dolls found attached to this and other pre-Inca mummy bundles. They may have been good luck charms used to ward off evil spirits, or they may have just been ornamentation.

The royal mummies had to be destroyed. They were objects of pagan worship and symbolic of Inca rule. In order to completely conquer the country and its people, Pizarro and his legions had to wipe out the pagan religion and the worship of Inca rulers. The people had to be forced to embrace Christianity and Spanish rule.

So, when the bodies of the Inca Emperors were found by Polo de Ondegardo in 1559, the royal mummies were systematically destroyed by the Spaniards. It is a pity that sixteenth-century Spanish writers were not more enthusiastic about recording the historical events of that time. However, there was one writer, Garcilaso Inca de la Vega, the son of one of the invaders and related to Inca royalty on his mother's side, who did set down a somewhat biased report.

He tells us that the Indians tried to save the royal mummies by hiding them from the Spaniards. But the Spaniards searched them out. He tells us that when a royal mummy was burned by the conquerors, its ashes were pitifully gathered up by the Indians and worshipped as fervently as the mummy itself had been.

Of course the Spaniards won out, and the Indians, in order to survive, pretended to convert to Catholicism. They were ingenious, though, and continued to carry out their old and elaborate ceremonies, telling the Spaniards that these rites were their adaptation of Christian rituals. For the Andeans, their royal mummies were never forgotten, and some of their ancient pagan symbols and customs are still present today.

Just as the dry, desert atmosphere of the Peruvian coast can preserve bodies, so have caves, in various parts of the world, been a natural environment for the protection of human remains.

The Cave of the Capuchins in Palermo, Sicily, is

one of the most famous of these and is, indeed, a great tourist attraction today. This cave has a cool, even temperature and is very dry. Over a period of years it was the custom to place the bodies of monks from nearby monasteries in the cave. Today, still clad in their monk's robes, and placed upright against the walls, others lying as if asleep on tiers of bunks, they remain quite well-preserved and present a fairly lifelike, if somewhat gruesome, appearance.

Here in the United States we often hear of American Indian mummies found in caves. Mammoth Cave and others in the limestone country of Kentucky and Tennessee have areas that are particularly favorable for preserving bodies.

In some of these—where Indian bodies lay in a state of good preservation for hundreds of years before being discovered—there are natural vaults, high and impressive, where the air circulates but stays steadily at a temperature just over 50 degrees. This in itself makes a fine atmosphere for the preservation of a body. But in addition, the dry floors of these caves have thin deposits of chemicals which aid in drying out and preserving bodies. In some caves the deposits are calcium nitrate. In others the chemical is magnesium sulfate. In either case the chemicals are effective.

Unlike the Capuchin monks, whose bodies were purposely placed in the caves for preservation, it is probable that most of the Indians found were victims of accident or sudden death and were trapped in the cave. One old man—a pre-Columbian Indian (that is, one who lived before Columbus discovered America)—had been trapped beneath a large limestone boulder. His left arm was badly fractured, but the body was fairly well-preserved, and remnants of the woven blanket he had worn still partly covered him.

However, not all Indian mummies were in their cave graves by accident. In a cave not far from Fort Casper, Wyoming, was found the preserved body of a man who had obviously been buried there on purpose.

The cave, formed in a sheer rock cliff along Poison Spider Creek, held the body of a man who had probably been of great importance, as it had been placed in the burial chamber with care and ceremony. The body was carefully balanced in a kneeling position, the hands crossed against his lower chest. He was not a young man, as his long hair was streaked with gray. He wore a collar of quills fashioned from the feathers of a large bird. No attempt at embalming had been made; there were no preservatives on his skin, no internal organs had been removed. His preservation was probably due entirely to the even, dry temperature of the cave, although the rocks in and around the cave contained petroleum, which might have had some chemical effect in preservation.

The discovery of Eskimo mummies is not surprising, since bodies in that land of ice and subzero temperatures may literally be kept preserved in cold storage.

But on one small Aleutian island the inhabitants,

for centuries, preserved their dead in caves with heat, not cold. Volcanic action deep in the earth beneath the caves generated so much heat that the burial caves maintained a high, even temperature. When placed in the caves, the dead were rapidly and effectively dried out, and mummified bodies, probably of great age, are still excellently preserved there.

Even when the Aleuts depended on cold for preserving their dead, they sometimes embalmed the bodies. As early as 1790 a traveler to the Aleutian Islands from the United States wrote a description of the natives of Unalaska and their treatment of their dead. "They pay respect to the memory of the dead; for they embalm the bodies with dried moss and grass," he wrote. A few years later another traveler wrote that the Aleuts removed the viscera from the body of the dead and filled the abdominal cavity with sweet dried hay to help preserve it.

One of the great collections of natural mummies in the world today is in the Mexican city of Guanajuato. Set in the midst of towering mountains, Guanajuato has a climate that alternates hot and cold. Yet its atmosphere is very dry and highly rarefied.

For centuries it has been customary to place the dead, unembalmed, in crypts in covered tiers aboveground, where they dry out, achieving in Guanajuato's special climate, natural mummification. Space in the tiers, though, is allotted for a specific length of time. When the time is up, the body, if unclaimed, is

165

moved to an underground chamber and space in the aboveground crypt is given to another, more recent corpse.

This practice has led to the accumulation of a great number of mummies in the underground sepulcher. There they stand, propped up, naked, row on row, preserved in quite lifelike form, to be stared at by the curious. It is quite possible for a resident of the town and surrounding countryside to come look at a relative or ancestor and, perhaps, muse that someday he too may have a place in the long row of mummies.

While the preservation of most bodies throughout the world has relied on favorable climatic conditions, usually a dry atmosphere, there are examples of the preservation of bodies under opposite conditions.

A collection of natural mummies in the underground chamber of the Pantheon of Guanajuato.

Among these are the well-preserved bodies found in certain peat bogs, mostly in northwestern Europe and the British Isles. The waters of these bogs contain acids that preserved the bodies through a kind of pickling process. The peat bogs of Denmark have yielded more of these bodies than those of any other country, and the whole dramatic story is told by a Danish archeologist, Dr. P. V. Glob, in his 1969 book, *The Bog People.*

How did the people get in the bogs? Of course a few wandered in, lost in darkness and storms, and died there. A few were murdered and their bodies hidden in the bogs. But most of the bodies found in Denmark, Holland, Germany, and other countries of northwestern Europe had been placed there by design and had certain things in common.

They were all naked, though sometimes a cap or a hood covered the head. They had all been in the bogs almost two thousand years, having lived in the Iron Age in the early centuries A.D. And, it appears, they had all been executed. Dr. Glob believes they had probably been sacrificed in pagan religious rites.

The finds were made over the last two hundred years, right up until modern times. Most of them were found by peasants and farmers, cutting peat for their fires. Unfortunately, only those discovered in recent years have been preserved and protected in museums. Earlier bodies were destroyed when well-meaning laymen felt the decent thing to do was to give the deceased a Christian burial in the village

The Grauballe man still embedded in the peat bog. Courtesy of P. V. Glob's *The Bog People* and The Forhistorisk Museum, Denmark.

churchyard. But, fortunately, in many cases detailed records were made of these finds. Thus, though the bodies disintegrated after being buried a second time, information on their appearance when found, the position of the bodies, and other data are available. By examining these records, Dr. Glob and other scientists could also tell which of these bodies were those of Iron Age men and women.

Some of the bog bodies were so perfectly preserved, the peat diggers finding them thought the body was a recent murder victim and went straight to the police. Luckily, for many years now the officials of even the smallest villages have known enough to leave the body in place and contact the nearest museum for professional help.

In at least three cases of recent finds even the stomach and intestinal tracts were so well-preserved that scientists could make a food analysis of their

The Tollund man, who died two thousand years ago. Courtesy of the National Museum of Denmark, Copenhagen.

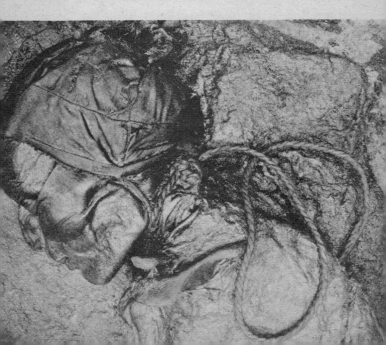

contents and determine what the men's last meal had been. Though these three may have lived and died a hundred years or more apart, their last meals had been the same: a kind of gruel made of dried seeds of weeds, flowers, and grasses.

They all had died in the winter or early spring, as there were no traces of berries or fruits, available in spring, summer, and fall. This led to the theory that they had been sacrificed in rites to the goddess of fertility—held in very early spring before the crops were planted—and symbolically their last meal consisted of seeds.

Two of these men had been hanged or strangled, and the rope nooses were still around their necks. The third had had his throat slit. Other Iron Age bodies found had died in these same ways, and reports left by earlier finders of bodies reburied told, too, of slit throats and necks wearing rope or leather nooses.

Not all the Iron Age people found gave evidence of sacrificial deaths. In Holland a naked young woman was found in a bog, a loose leather collar around her neck and a bandage drawn over her eyes. She had probably been buried alive in the bog as punishment for adultery. This was deduced because her head was shaved—a mark in her day of a convicted adulteress. Examination of the body, including radiographs, showed she was only fourteen years old. And there were no marks or signs of violence on the body that could have caused her death. It was assumed that she had been led, naked and blindfolded, to the peat pit and drowned in the watery bog, as a large stone was placed against one side of her body and the body was covered with birch branches, as if to weight it down.

In Sweden a farmer cutting peat came upon the body of a well-dressed, well-preserved gentleman who had been murdered six hundred years before. His distinctive dress told the Swedish scholar who examined him that he had lived around 1350. Death had been caused by a vicious blow on the side of the head. After placing him in the bog, his murderers had driven an oak stake into his heart, through his body, pinning him down in the bog. There was a superstition at the time that if this was done, a person's ghost could not walk and thus torment those who had killed him.

In England, on a winter night in 1675, a young man and his girl were lost in a snowstorm and drowned in a bog. The following spring the bodies were found. It was decided to rebury them, together, in the bog where they had met death. Years later a villager, curious, opened the double grave and found the bodies, lifelike and perfectly preserved. It is said that for several years afterward the young pair were exhibited at county fairs—until descendants of the girl's family put a stop to the ghoulish business and gave the young couple a decent burial.

In all, it has been estimated that more than six

hundred bodies have been taken from peat bogs in Denmark, Germany, Holland, Sweden, Norway, and the British Isles. Some were in remarkably fine condition. Others were so poorly preserved, they could not even be dated.

Of all those that could be dated, by far the greatest number go back to the Iron Age, just before and in the early centuries of the Christian Era. This is because the later bog victims were less numerous to begin with. They were victims of accidental drowning; perhaps a few were murdered. When they disappeared, friends and family searched for them. The bodies found, they were taken from the bog and buried in a cemetery or graveyard.

But the Iron Age men and women were victims of execution. Placed in their watery graves on purpose, they were meant to stay there. They must have been numerous indeed.

Scientifically the bog bodies are of special interest because they are the only examples of body preservation by nature that did not depend on cold or heat, dry air, a rarefied atmosphere, an even temperature, or a combination of these. They were preserved only because of the quality of the bog water and their lack of exposure to air.

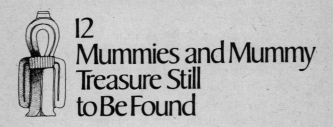

12
Mummies and Mummy Treasure Still to Be Found

There is a mummy of a famous ancient Egyptian that archeologists still hope to find in Egypt. His name is Imhotep. He was a vizier, or what we today might call prime minister, to the Pharaoh Zoser (also known as Djoser), who ruled in the 3rd Dynasty, almost five thousand years ago.

Imhotep wielded great power and was famous in his own day as an architect and builder, a scholar, and a physician. Even after his death his fame grew and eventually he was thought of as the god of medicine, thus achieving a measure of deification.

A man as powerful as he, trusted by the Pharaoh, revered by the people, would have had a magnificent burial. So far no tomb, no sarcophagus bearing his name, has been found.

And yet, somewhere he must lie, possibly in all the splendor with which he was buried and resting in a coffin of gold. Everyone who wants to be an archeologist must surely dream of making such a find. And perhaps someone will.

To some extent the archeologist of the future may be helped by modern science and inventions. For example, Egyptologists for years have suspected that there may be additional rooms, still undiscovered and unexplored, hidden in the depths of the pyramids. All attempts to find clues to new passages have failed. But recently scientists have begun cosmic-ray studies, which they hope may reveal the presence of "lost" rooms in the pyramids.

With a cosmic-ray detector it is possible to record the amount of cosmic radiation at any given point in a pyramid. The amount of radiation that is absorbed tells the scientists if they are encountering a space area, such as a room, or if the area is solid stone.

They began their studies with Khufu's Great Pyramid at Giza. At first the equipment was installed in a small unfinished room *under* the pyramid. Later it was moved higher up, into a room known as the Queen's Chamber, where work is still in progress. The job is far from finished, and there are other pyramids waiting to be studied.

In a structure as huge as the Great Pyramid at Giza, a tremendous number of recordings must be made. This time-consuming task is eased somewhat by feeding all the findings into a computer, which can map the hollow areas.

The computer should speed up a number of once tedious jobs for the modern archeologist. But it doesn't always work.

Over a period of years thousands and thousands of large stones on which scenes were carved were found in the temple ruins of Karnak and Luxor. Approximately 100,000 of these blocks have been discovered, and it is obvious that the scenes are continuous. Thus if the stones could ever be put in proper sequence, they would have long and exciting stories to tell.

In 1966, Ray Winfield Smith from the University of Pennsylvania and his friend, Anwar Shoukry, Director General of the Department of Antiquities of Egypt, met. Ray thought Anwar the perfect scholar to bring some order to the chaos of blocks; Anwar thought Ray eminently qualified. Shortly thereafter, with funds from the Smithsonian Institution, the two began the awesome task of arranging them in sequence. This seemed a logical place for a computer to be of help. But it proved too slow and unwieldy. Finally it was decided to let people do the job, by eye. Small pictures were made of each stone and these are

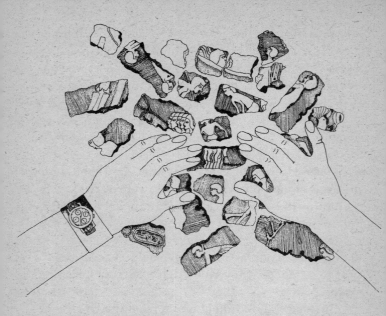

Pictures were taken of the many stones found in the temple ruins of Karnak and Luxor and made into a giant jigsawpuzzle.

now set out on long tables—a seemingly endless, giant jigsaw puzzle which teams of young men and women are trying to place in proper order.

But in spite of all the help possible from modern devices, the work of the archeologist will always be hard and at times unpleasant. For treasures are where you find them and often the sites are difficult to reach.

Sir William M. Flinders Petrie, the famous English archeologist, told of finally discovering the hidden tomb of the great noble, Horuta. It remained a secret because the massive limestone sarcophagus had been placed in a small chamber, off a large chamber, deep down a straight shaft, which had then been solidly filled up with masonry so the existence of the tomb would not be suspected. It lay forty feet deep, and the chamber was half-filled with black water. Over a period of months, bit by bit, the masonry was cut away.

The stone lid block of the sarcophagus, which was almost under water, was two feet thick, and weeks were spent in the dark, wet chamber cutting this into small pieces and lifting it out. Petrie tells of sitting astride the sarcophagus, trying to remove the coffin lid, "unable to turn my head without tasting the bitter brine in which I sat."

He managed to get the first coffin lid off, but the second coffin—and, as it turned out, a third one—was not only under stagnant water but imbedded in sand. Said he, "The need of doing everything by feeling under the black water made it slow business." At long last the nesting coffins were loosened, ropes were attached, and the coffins hauled above the surface of the water into the chamber.

The mummy of Horuta yielded exquisite jewelry of gold, statuettes delicately carved of semiprecious stones, and the richest and most complete set of amulets ever seen intact. But even the dedicated Petrie admitted the task of retrieving them had been brutally hard and most unpleasant.

On the other hand, sometimes the treasure lays almost within sight and makes the finder giddy with the chance discovery. Herbert E. Winlock, an American Egyptologist, was with the Metropolitan Museum Expedition in western Thebes. One day a workman was sweeping up small scraps from a long corridor that had yielded nothing and which Winlock was about to abandon. Then it was noticed that small chips of stone seemed to be falling down a crack. Winlock lay upon the floor and shone his flashlight into the crack. Describing his experience later, he wrote:

The beam of light shot into a little world of four thousand years ago, and I was gazing down into the midst of a myriad of brightly painted little men going this way and that.

A tall slender girl gazed across at me, perfectly composed; a gang of little men with sticks in their upraised hands drove spotted oxen; rowers tugged at their oars on a fleet of boats, while one ship seemed floundering right in front of me with its bow balanced precariously in the air. And all of this busy going and coming was in uncanny silence, as though the distance back over the forty centuries I looked across was too great for even an echo to reach my ears.

Winlock had found a large and beautiful cache of perfectly preserved models carved of wood that showed the Egyptians going about their daily tasks in the 11th Dynasty, almost 2,000 years before Christ. They had been placed in the tomb of a nobleman, Meket-Re, to accompany him into the next world, assuring that he might enjoy every possible needed service in eternity. There were men busy in the carpenter shop, the brewery, the butcher shop; women weaving and spinning cloth for him; the granary, his yacht, his fishing boats with men at the oars; young girls carrying baskets of food—all in exquisite detail and proportion.

Not only were these prized for their beauty. They gave a wealth of information about how the Egyptians lived in that long-ago era.

We can imagine the archeologist's joy and excitement, peering down the crack and seeing this great treasure. But was it as "chancy" as it sounds? The area he had been working on had been excavated twice before by archeologists and abandoned when nothing was found. Winlock wondered if they might have overlooked something.

And they had. It was persistent hard work and the good archeologist's power of observation, obsession with detail, that led him to the prize.

Even after a successful find is made, sometimes the amount of work that lies ahead is prodigious. When George Reisner and his Harvard-Boston team found the tomb of Queen Hetepheres, its floor piled and littered with sheets and strips of gold and scraps of decayed wood, it took twenty years of painstaking work to fit everything back together again and reconstruct the queen's golden furniture.

When we see the great wealth of treasures that have been discovered in Egypt, we wonder if there are many exciting discoveries left to be made by future archeologists.

Yes, there are. Right now there is a large pit within the enclosure wall that surrounds the Great Pyramid of Giza waiting to be opened.

In 1952 men were clearing accumulations of sand away from a terrace between the wall and the south side of the pyramid. They came upon large limestone slabs that covered what apparently was a big pit. The pit was about 120 feet long and boat-shaped; that is, tapered at the ends. As they cleared more sand away, they came upon a second pit, same size, same shape, also covered with limestone slabs.

When the first pit was opened, they found a great travel boat that had belonged to the Pharaoh Khufu, builder of the Great Pyramid. The boat had, somehow, miraculously survived its centuries buried in the earth without termite damage or wood rot. And, being larger than the 120 foot pit, it had been completely dismantled in order to fit into the long, boat-shaped excavation.

There were hundreds of pieces, large and small. But before they removed a single piece of the boat, a building known as a reconstruction shelter had to be built and equipped for the big job of putting the boat back together again. The reconstruction of the boat was finally completed in 1972—twenty years after discovery of the pit. Meantime, a museum had been built over the pit to house the boat and properly display it.

Because of the prevailing winds, boats going south on the Nile had sails. Boats traveling north were rowed by men. Since this boat had no mast, it was clearly Khufu's boat for northward travel.

So far the second pit has not been opened. But it will be. Elaborate plans are being made for doing a thoroughly scientific job of it. Among other things, scientists are exploring ways of studying the atmosphere within the pit before uncovering it. They then will try to reproduce the atmosphere so that whatever the pit may hold will not be damaged. The archeologists feel they were lucky in excavating the first pit without damage to the boat. They want no chances taken on the second.

They ask, what will we find? Will it be another

This drawing is adapted from Björn Landström's expert reconstruction of Khufu's traveling boat found dismantled in the
first pit.

great travel boat of Khufu's, this one with a mast and sails for travel southward? Or will the pit be empty, the boat, once there, destroyed by termites? And then again, it may not contain a boat at all, but treasures of another kind.

Among the places future archeologists will find interesting and rewarding to dig are the oases of Egypt. Some of these, green and fertile areas surrounded by desert, are large in size and were thriving communities in ancient Egypt. As far back as the Old Kingdom, 2686–2181 B.C., many of them existed under direct control of the Pharaohs and continued through succeeding dynasties to be important principalities of the kings. Though today the oases are populated mostly by seminomadic tribes, for centuries they enjoyed, under the rule of the Pharaohs, the advantages of ancient Egyptian culture. Evidence of those centuries surely lies buried there.

While some excavating has been done in the oases, it has not been undertaken systematically. So there are areas largely unexplored where finds are waiting to be made.

But let the aspiring archeologist be warned! The climate is hot. Scorching winds blow in from the surrounding desert. And one young American student reports that the mosquitoes are the size of sparrows.

However, there are those who feel that living

with such discomforts is a small price to pay for the opportunity to search and discover.

And you will find mummies!

In the summer of 1972 a team digging in the Fayum, one of the larger oases, came upon a splendid cache of mummies, all minor royalty, each still wearing its handsome gilded mask. Archeologically these oases are very important.

One official in the Department of Antiquities in Cairo said there was still so much treasure to be found that if he could, he would invite all the young archeologists in every university in the world to come to Egypt and dig!

Bibliography

Aldred, Cyril, *The Egyptians*, Thames and Hudson, London, 1965.

Baikie, James, *A Century of Excavation in the Land of the Pharaohs*, The Religious Tract Society, London, 1924.

——, *Egyptian Antiquities in the Nile Valley*, Methuen & Co., London, 1932.

Baumann, Bill B., M.D. "The botanical aspects of ancient Egyptian embalming and burial", *Economic Botany*, Vol. 14, pp. 84–104, New York Botanical Garden, New York, 1960.

Breasted, James H., *A History of Egypt* (Charles Scribner's Sons, 1905), Bantam Books Edition, New York, 1967.

Budge, E. A. W., *The Mummy: A Handbook of Egyptian Funerary Archaeology*, Cambridge University Press, 1925.

Cerny, J., *Egypt: From the Death of Ramesses III to the End of the Twenty-First Dynasty*, Cambridge University Press, Fascicle #27, 1965.

Ciba Symposia, "Embalming," Vol. 6, May 1944.

Dawson, W. R., "Making a Mummy," Journal of Egyptian Archaeology, Vol. 13, 1927.

——, "Mummification in Australia and America," Royal Anthropological Institute of Great Britain, Vol. 58, 1928.

———, "Pettigrew's Demonstrations upon Mummies," Journal of Egyptian Archaeology, Vol. 20, 1934.

———, and Gray, P. H. K., *Mummies and Human Remains*, Catalogue of Egyptian Antiquities in the British Museum I, London, 1968.

———, and Smith, G. E., *Egyptian Mummies*, Dial Press, New York, 1924.

Edwards, I. E. S., Gadd, C. J., and Hammond, N. G. D., *The Cambridge Ancient History*, Vol. 1, Parts 1 and 2, 3rd Edition, Cambridge University Press, London, 1970.

Emery, Walter B., *Archaic Egypt*, Penguin Books, London, 1961.

Faulkner, R. O., *Egypt: From the Inception of the Nineteenth Dynasty to the Death of Ramesses III*, Cambridge University Press, Fascicle #52, 1966.

Fox, Penelope, *Tutankhamen's Treasure*, Oxford University Press, 1961.

Gardiner, Sir Alan H., *The Attitude of the Ancient Egyptians to Death and the Dead*, Cambridge University Press, 1935.

Garstang, John, *The Burial Customs of Ancient Egypt*, Archibald Constable & Co., London, 1907.

Glob, P. V., *The Bog People*, Cornell University Press, 1969.

Gray, P. H. K., and Slow, D., "Egyptian Mummies in the City of Liverpool Museums," Liverpool, Liverpool Corporation, 1968, (Liverpool Museum Bulletin No. 15.).

Harris, J. E., and Weeks, K. R., *X-raying the Pharaohs*, Charles Scribner's Sons, New York, 1972.

Hayes, William C., *Egypt: From the Death of Ammenemes III to Seqenenre II*, Cambridge University Press, Fascicle #6, 1965.

Hemming, John, *The Conquest of the Incas*, Harcourt, Brace, Jovanovich, New York, 1970.

Herodotus, *The Histories*, Penguin Books, Baltimore, 1965.

James, T. G. H., *Egypt: From the Expulsion of the Hyksos to Amenophis I*, Cambridge University Press, Fascicle #34, 1965.

Lucas, Alfred, *Ancient Egyptian Materials and Industries*, 4th Edition, St. Martins Press, London, 1962.

———, "The Use of Natron in Mummification," Journal of Egyptian Archaeology, Vol. 18, 1932.

Martin, R. A., *Mummies*, Field Museum of Natural History Popular Series #36, Chicago, 1969.

Maspero, Sir Gaston, *Manual of Egyptian Archaeology*, 3rd Edition, G. P. Putnam's Sons, New York, 1892.

McCracken, Harold, *God's Frozen Children*, Doubleday, New York, 1930.

Migliarini, A. M., "Account of the Unrolling of a Mummy at Florence, Belonging to the Grand Duke of Tuscany," trans. by C. H. Cottrell, *Archaeologia*, Vol. 36, 1855.

Noblecourt, C. Desroches, *Tutankhamen*, New York Graphic Society, New York, 1963.

Pettigrew, Thomas J., *A History of Egyptian Mummies*, Longman, Rees, London, 1834.

Petrie, Sir William M. Flinders, *Ten Years Digging in Egypt 1881–1891*, Oxford, 1893.

———, *Seventy Years in Archaeology*, S. Low, Marston & Co., London, 1931.

Reisner, G. A., and Smith, W. S., *A History of the Giza Necropolis*, Vol. 2, Harvard University Press, Cambridge, Mass.; Oxford University Press, H. Milford, London, 1955.

Rowe, John Howland, "Inca Culture at the Time of the Spanish Conquest", pgs. 183–330 in the Smithsonian Institution Bureau of American Ethnology Bulletin 143, *Handbook of South American Indians*, Julian H. Steward, Editor, Vol. 2, The Andean Civilization, Washington, 1946.

Ruffer, Sir Marc A., *Studies in the Paleopathology of Ancient Egypt*, University of Chicago Press, Chicago, 1921.

Sameh, Waley-el-dine, *Daily Life of Ancient Egypt*, McGraw-Hill, New York, 1964.

Smith, G. E., *A Contribution to the Study of Mummification*. (Mémoires présentés à l'Institut Egyptien, tome V, 1906.).

———, "Egyptian Mummies," Journal of Egyptian Archaeology, Vol. I, 1914.

———, *The Royal Mummies*, Cairo Institut Français d'archéologie orientale, 1912 (Catalogue général des antiquités Egyptiennes du Musée du Cairo, Nos. 61051–61100.).

———, and Jones, F. W., *The Archaeological Survey of Nubia 1907–1908, Vol. II, Report on the Human Remains*, National Printing Department, Cairo, 1910.

Smith, W. S., *The Art and Architecture of Ancient Egypt*, Penguin History of Art, Baltimore, 1965.

Wilson, John A., *Signs and Wonders upon a Pharaoh*, University of Chicago Press, Chicago, 1964.

Winlock, Herbert E., *Excavations at Dier el Bahri, 1911–1931*, The MacMillan Co., New York, 1942.

———, *Models of Daily Life in Ancient Egypt*, Metropolitan Museum of Art, Publication V 18, New York, 1955.

Index

191